Amazing Insects

The Secret World of Invertebrates

Published in 2009 by New Holland Publishers
London • Cape Town • Sydney • Auckland
www.newhollandpublishers.com

Garfield House, 86-88 Edgware Road, London W2 2EA, UK
80 McKenzie Street, Cape Town, 8001, South Africa
Unit 1, 66 Gibbes Street, Chatswood, NSW 2067, Australia
218 Lake Road, Northcote, Auckland, New Zealand

1 3 5 7 9 10 8 6 4 2

ISBN 978 1 84773 516 4

Although the publishers have made every effort to ensure that information contained in this book was meticulously researched and correct at the time of going to press, they accept no responsibility for any inaccuracies, loss, injury or inconvenience sustained by any person using this book as reference.

Publisher: Simon Papps
Publishing Director: Rosemary Wilkinson
Translator: Joseph Muise
Editor: Marianne Taylor
Layout: Tammy Warren

Printed in China. ✪

Amazing Insects

The Secret World of Invertebrates

PHOTOGRAPHY BY JEAN-CLAUDE TEYSSIER

TEXT BY JEAN-HENRI FABRE

NEW
HOLLAND

Biodiversity is a Treasure

By Hubert Reeves

Astrophysicist

It is not the size of a living being that determines its importance. Perhaps even the reverse is true. We cannot attribute a species's worth to its size, since all species have a role to play on our blue planet.

Without insects, the planet could not easily rid itself of the dead wood on the forest floor, or the cowpats in its fields... without them, there would be no bees busy pollinating flowers and the diversity of our flora would be reduced. This natural biodiversity is a treasure, and each living species is part of it.

It is through nature's artistry that we have gained this incredibly rich biodiversity. In much the same way, the human artist mimics nature by contributing to the artistic wealth of the world. Each of Jean-Claude Teyssier's photos is proof of this — capturing the wonder of the insect while letting it be free.

Preface

Of all the creatures that live on Earth, insects are among the most hated, feared and despised. We refer to them as 'bugs' or 'creepy-crawlies.' Humans put a great deal of effort into trying to eliminate them with insecticides and pesticides, in what amounts to extreme, zero-tolerance warfare.

It is perhaps easy to ignore the fact that these arthropods are among the oldest, most numerous, best adapted, and most useful of creatures to both man and nature. Without them, the Earth would not be as it is. Even if an urge to destroy insects is part of our nature, who are we to decide that a being should not survive solely on account of its small size? Every life has meaning, inherent value and justification. The insect that we want to crush may be a father, a mother or an important part of a wider community.

Life is big, beautiful and noble. For its sake we undertake hugely costly interplanetary space explorations in the hopes of discovering the slightest trace of life on other worlds. So far all of these expeditions have come back empty-handed — as far as we know at the moment, Earth is the only planet that enjoys the gift of life.

It is, therefore, with great honour that I write the preface for this work that showcases an important component of life on Earth: insects. The author, through his original choice of species, his scientific rigour and his beautiful photographs, which pair so beautifully with Jean-Henri Fabre's texts, has made a valuable and generous contribution to the entomological literature.

From the bottom of my heart, I thank you for your contribution to popularizing and educating on this important topic, and reconciling our relationships with a class of animals from which we could learn a great deal: insects. The result is a 'blockbuster' of entomological photography.

Georges Brossard
Notary and Entomologist
Founder of the Montreal Insectarium

Contents

Female conehead mantis (*Empusa pennata*) on flowers of ligularia.

Spring

spring

Immature Great Green Bush Cricket (*Tettigonia viridissima*) on an Ox-eye Daisy.

This is how it went. There were five or six of us: me, their teacher, companion and friend; and them, young, enthusiastic and overflowing with imagination from the spring-like sap of life that sparks our desire to learn. Talking about this and that, we walked along a path bordered with hawthorn, where the Rose Chafer beetle was enjoying the bitter smells of the hawthorn in bloom.

We were going to see if the Scarab Beetle had made its first appearance at the sandy plateau to roll its ball of dung, an image that was meant to represent the world in Ancient Egypt. We were also interested to see if we could find young newts, with gills like feathery branches of coral, under the duckweed in the running water at the base of the hill... or if the elegant stream-dwelling sticklebacks had developed their crimson and azure breeding colours; if the newly arrived Swallow was skimming across the grassland on its pointed wings, or if the crane-flies were laying their eggs and dancing. We wondered if at the opening of a burrow carved in the sandstone a jewelled Sand Lizard would be sunning itself; if the Black-headed Gull, coming from the sea in search of the schools of fish that travel up the Rhône to lay their eggs in its waters, could be found gliding in noisy groups along the river, filling the air with a sound not unlike fanatical laughter; if... Let's leave it at that. In essence, simple people that we are, taking great pleasure in living with nature's creatures, we were spending the morning celebrating the ineffable awakening of life that spring brings.

Pair of Butterfly-lions
(*Libelloides coccajus*) on a stalk of grass.

garden and wasp spiders

BEE BEETLE (*Trichodes alvearius*) on an Ox-eye Daisy.

Like plant seeds, many insects and their relatives have means of travel and dispersal that enable them to quickly spread throughout the countryside, allowing each to have its place in the sun. These evolutionary devices can compete with the ingenuity developed by the elm tree and the dandelion in spreading their seed.

Let's now consider the web-spinning spiders. These superb spiders hang a large vertical mesh of silk from one bush to another, not unlike that of a bird-catcher. The most remarkable example near my home is the Wasp Spider (*Argiope bruennichi*), with its lovely yellow, black and silver stripes. Its nest is a satin sac in the shape of a pear, with a concave opening at the end of the neck on which is set a small satin lid. Brown ribbons decorate the nest from one end to the other. Let's open the nest. Under the outer layer, which is as strong and resilient as our finest fabrics as well as being water-resistant, sits an exquisite red duvet. No mother could prepare a softer bed.

At the centre of this soft mass, hangs a small purse of silk in the shape of a thimble with a moveable cover. It is here that the spider encloses its beautiful orange-yellow eggs, which number roughly 500.

YOUNG GARDEN SPIDERS (*Araneus diadematus*)

Lily Bush Cricket (*Tylopsis liliifolia*)
on a scabious flower.

garden and wasp spiders | ||

Wasp Spider (*Argiope bruennichi*) wrapping up a Lily Bush Cricket.

All things considered, this elegant egg-carrying structure is the equivalent of a fruit or a seed pod, a container of new life comparable to those of the plant world. The Wasp Spider's sac contains eggs rather than seeds, but the difference is not so important, since an egg and a seed are essentially the same.

How will the opening of this living fruit that has ripened in the heat much-loved by cicadas unfold? How will the hatching and dispersal take place? There will soon be hundreds of baby spiders. They must separate themselves, and each make the long journey to a new home, isolated from each other so that they do not compete for food or space. How will they undertake this mass exodus in their delicate state?

The first answer I get comes from another, more familiar spider, whose family I find on some Bear Grass in the paddock at the beginning of May. The plant had flowered last year. Atop its flowering oar-shaped stalk sit the untouched, dried remnants of its flowers. On its green leaves, like sword blades, the recently hatched babies are busy making their way up. The minute creatures are pale yellow in colour, with a triangular spot on the rump. Later, this will develop into a triple white cross, confirming that these are indeed Garden Spiders (*Araneus diadematus*).

With the sun shifting to the corner of the paddock, one of the two groups is showing signs of fresh activity. Agile acrobats that they are, the small spiders climb one after the other to reach the top of the flowering head. Here they seem to walk backwards and forwards, the blowing wind causing disorder and confusion amongst the group. I cannot easily distinguish their movements. However, one by one, they take flight from the flowering head. One would think that they had the wings of a midge.

common froghopper

COMMON FROGHOPPER (*Philaenus spumarius*) in its foam nest under an Ox-eye Daisy.

With the arrival of the Swallow and the Cuckoo in April, let's look to the fields, first surveying the ground, like all careful observers of the insect world. We cannot miss the small blobs of white foam that dot the pasture. These could be mistaken for the frothy spit of a passer-by, but their sheer numbers make this theory implausible. Human saliva could not rise to such frothy heights, however hard the spitter might try.

In spite of their knowledge that humans play no part in the creation of the foam masses, the countryside people have retained this description based on appearances. They refer to the foamy blobs as 'cuckoo spit', in honour of the bird whose song signals the arrival of spring. The migratory bird spits it out in flight, they say, while searching for the nests of other birds to find a place to lay its eggs.

Do we want to know the real source of these frothy masses? With a piece of straw, let's have a poke about in the foam. We extract from it a large-bellied, stocky, yellow bug, resembling a cicada without its wings. This is the worker who is behind the foam.

MARSH FRITILLARY BUTTERFLY (*Euphydryas aurinia*)
on an Ox-eye Daisy.

PAIR OF MARSH FRITILLARIES (*Euphydryas aurinia*)

When we place it on another leaf, the bug waves the pointed end of its plump belly in an oscillating up-and-down movement, producing new foam. In a few days we will see this creature in a slightly changed form. Older and still busy maintaining its foamy cover, the insect moults and grows, changes colour to green and grows stumps of wings that stick like sashes to its flanks. From its head juts out a small tendril, a beak analogous to that of a cicada, which it uses as a sucker to draw sap from the plant. Those entomologists happy to use informal nomenclature accurately call this species 'Spittlebug'.

Inside each nest of foam, you will typically find just one froghopper (though there are sometimes two, three or more – usually resulting from the unintended joining of individual nests to form a shared home). Let's observe the beginnings of the work. Armed with a magnifying glass, we can follow the construction process. The sucker implanted up to the base and its six short legs well anchored, the froghopper is motionless, its belly flat against the leaf where it sits. If we ask ourselves what advantages the froghopper gains from its mass of froth, very plausible answers quickly come to mind: under this cover,

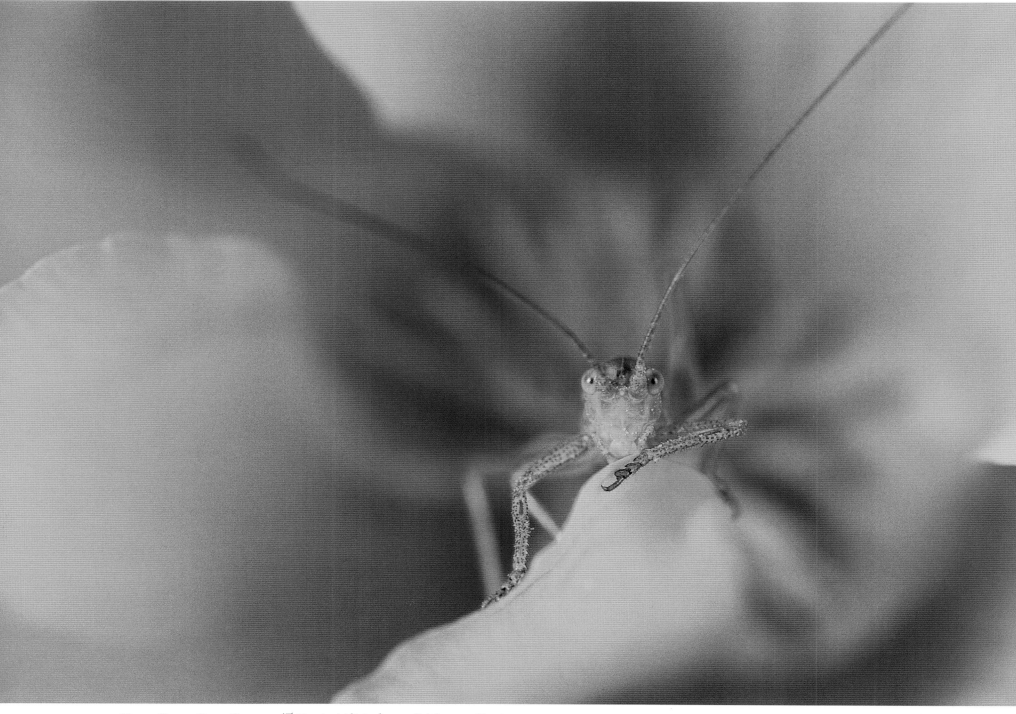

GREAT GREEN BUSH CRICKET (*Tettigonia viridissima*) on a Californian Poppy.

the insect remains cool, can evade the gaze of predators, and avoids the bright sun and parasites. In truth, as a defence system, the foam housing is a terrific invention.

The insect only emerges from its frothy home when it reaches adulthood in the form of a cute, brown-coloured cicada-like bug. Highly skilled at escaping its predators, it can make large and sudden leaps (hence 'froghopper'), sending it far from its aggressors, and making its life considerably easier.

Butterfly from the Satyridae family drinking nectar from an Ox-eye Daisy.

Honey Bees (*Apis mellifera*) at the entrance to the hive.

Honey Bee (*Apis mellifera*) on a poppy flower.

Incredibly social creature though it is, the Honey Bee does also have a streak of maternal selfishness. For each hive, there is only one single mother (the queen). If there are two, civil war breaks out. One will die from the other's stings, or alternatively she escapes, followed by a part of the hive. Despite being theoretically capable of laying eggs, the worker bees, numbering 20,000, relinquish parenthood and devote themselves to celibacy to serve the prodigious family of their mother, the queen. A similar way of life is pursued by many species of wasps, ants, termites and other social insects. This communal lifestyle in which thousands and thousands of individuals remain incomplete and become humble helpers to the sexually gifted few makes for an incredibly strong and productive colony. The moment that maternity is granted as a privilege to all, individualism resurfaces, as is the case with the Carpenter Bees which live alone or in loose social groups.

Honey Bee (*Apis mellifera*)
feeding from a Sage flower.

ADONIS BLUE BUTTERFLY (*Lysandra bellargus*)
on a grass head catching the last rays of sunshine.

HEATH FRITILLARY BUTTERFLY (*Mellicta athalia*)

young praying mantis

YOUNG PRAYING MANTISES (*Mantis religiosa*) emerging from the nest.

ADULT PRAYING MANTIS (*Mantis religiosa*)
on a Pomegranate flower.

YOUNG PRAYING MANTIS (*Mantis religiosa*) on a cornflower.

In the bright sunshine of a mid-June day, around ten o'clock in the morning, the hatching of Praying Mantis eggs takes place. The central strip or exit area is the only part of the nest from which the young can escape.

Under the outer layer in this area, we see a blunt protrusion slowly break through, followed by two black dots, which are the eyes. Delicately, the newborn slides out from under the strip and partially frees itself. Is this small mantis in its larval form very similar to an adult? Not yet. This is a transitional state. The head is opalescent and blunt, with palpitations caused by the influx of blood. The rest of its body is coloured a reddish-yellow. Its large black eyes, somewhat clouded by the veil that covers them, are still easily distinguishable. Its mouthparts are spread against its chest, and its last two pairs of legs glued to the body. To sum up, excepting its very noticeable front legs, on the whole, its large blunt head, dark eyes, fine abdominal segmentation and boat-like shape, are more reminiscent of a newborn cicada, a sort a miniature fish without fins. These babies do not spend much time on the nest. They let themselves fall or climb onto the neighbouring greenery. In less than 20 minutes it's all over. The abandoned nest that they shared will be left alone for a few days, only to be filled with another clutch of eggs, until the mother mantis's stock of eggs runs out.

On many occasions I have witnessed these mass exoduses,

YOUNG PRAYING MANTIS (*Mantis religiosa*) on a rose.

either in the open air of the paddock, where I have amassed an impressive collection of nests gathered during my winter leisure, or in the greenhouse, where I naively believed I could safeguard the newborn family. Nine times out of ten, when I witnessed the hatching, a scene of unforgettable carnage took place before my eyes. A female Praying Mantis can produce thousands of eggs in its rounded belly, in the hope that a few babies will survive the attentions of the many voracious predators that will attack them once they emerge from their eggs.

Ants are especially fierce in their attempts at exterminating them. It seems strange that the Praying Mantis – future killer of insects, the terrible hunter – is eaten at its birth by one of the least deadly of insects, the ant. However, this carnage does not last long. Once it has put on a little weight and its legs have become stronger and firmer, the mantis is no longer the target of attacks. Blithely it walks amongst the ants, who flee at its passing rather than attempting to attack it. Its front legs held close to its breast, like arms ready to box, it is already making its presence known with its proud stance.

YOUNG PRAYING MANTIS (*Mantis religiosa*)
on an iris leaf.

YOUNG PRAYING MANTIS (*Mantis religiosa*) with its prey (a bush cricket) on a rose.

The prolific mother mantis will one day become the organic matter that will be inherited by the ant, the songbird, or perhaps even humans. She leaves behind a thousand young, some to perpetuate herself, and many that will never survive to adulthood but instead contribute to the survival of other living things. She brings us back to the ancient symbol of the snake that bites its own tail – the world is a circle that meets itself. Everything finishes so that everything can start again. Everything dies in order that everything may live.

YOUNG BUISH CRICKET from the family Phaneropterinae on a rose petal.

bee beetle

BEE BEETLE (*Trichodes alvearius*) on a buttercup.

Three beetle larvae are acting as undertakers: a Bee Beetle, a Spider Beetle, and a skin beetle (family Dermestidae). They are making the most of the leftovers. The larvae of the skin beetle and the Spider Beetle are eating away the cadaverous detritus. The larva of the Bee Beetle, with its black head and pretty rose-coloured body, seems to be making its way through the old jars of rancid honey. The adult insect, image of perfection with its vermillion-coloured costume decorated in blue, is not a rare sight on the surface of overturned earth during the work season, slowly making its way through the fields to enjoy the drops of honey that seep from some cracked jars. Despite its conspicuous livery, so poorly matched with the drab frocks of worker bees, the Carpenter Bees let it be, as if they recognized in it the hygiene of a sewer worker.

conehead mantis

Wild meadow, flowering Pyramidal Orchid.

What to say about the Conehead Mantis? The insect world has few creatures as bizarre. Children, with their uncanny ability to come up with names that conjure precise images, call it the 'little devil.' It is alarming in appearance, a diabolical ghost with a haunting image. Its flattened stomach, cut out on the sides into garlands, sweeps up in a spiralling arch. Its conical head is crowned with two large diverging horns, not unlike spikes. Its fine pointed face, which is capable of looking sideways, lives up to several representations of Satan. Its long legs have small lamellar appendages at the joints, as if it were wearing armbands on its elbows like the fearless warriors of old. Lifted high on the stilts of its hind legs, with its convolutedly folded abdomen, thorax standing straight, its front legs, ready to trap, are folded neatly against its breast. Idly it stands balancing itself, wobbling on the end of a branch. To see it for the first time in its fantastic pose will make one jump with surprise.

YOUNG CONEHEAD MANTIS (*Empusa pennata*)
on a Sainfoin flower.

Left:
GREAT GREEN BUSH CRICKET (*Tettigonia viridissima*)
in a poppy flower.

Right:
CRAB SPIDER (*Thomisus* sp.)
on a poppy capsule.

Great Green Bush Cricket (*Tettigonia viridissima*) in a poppy flower.

POPPIES (*Papaver rhoeas*)
before the storm.

YOUNG BUSH CRICKET of the family Phaneropterinae
on a poppy petal.

BEE BEETLE (*Trichodes alvearius*)
on an iris flower.

YOUNG BUSH CRICKET of the Phaneropterinae
family balancing on a poppy petal.

GARDEN SNAIL (*Helix aspersa*)
at night, during a shower.

COMMON GLOW WORM LARVA (*Lampyris noctiluca*) feeding on a snail.

One could argue against calling this creature a 'worm' – do not be mistaken by its appearance, it is not a worm at all. It has six short legs that it can make very good use of, and uses to scurry around in small steps. When it reaches adulthood, the male is equipped with elytra (wing-cases), like the true beetle that it is. The female, however, is wingless and does not experience the joys of flight. Her life during the larval stage is identical to that of the male, who is as incomplete as her, until they reach sexual maturity and pair up.

Despite its modest appearance, the Common Glow Worm larva is in fact carnivorous, a hunter that conducts itself with rare villainy. Its standard prey is the snail. Before consuming its prey, the Glow Worm anaesthetizes its victim by injecting a toxin, not unlike in surgery, rendering its subject insensible to pain before operating on it. The typical prey is a small Garden Snail, no bigger than a cherry. In the summer, on the roadsides, such snails assemble in clusters on the stems of strong grasses, resting motionlessly, as long as the summer heat persists. It is in this position that I have, many a time, surprised a glow worm attached to the prey that it had just immobilised with its surgical tactics.

A singular feature of the glow worm is that its eggs are luminous, even when they are still inside the female. If I inadvertently crushed a female with a belly full of completely developed eggs, a glowing trail would spread on my fingers as if I had broken a vial filled with a phosphorescent fluid. The magnifying glass tells me that I am mistaken. The luminosity is due to the cluster of eggs violently expulsed from the female's body. The glow remains within the female – through the segments of the abdomen a soft opalescent luminosity appears. The hatch quickly follows after the egg-laying. The young, regardless of their sex, have two small dim lights in their final segments. With the bitter cold of winter approaching, they burrow into the earth, though not very deeply.

From beginning to end, the glow worm's life is one great orgy of light. The eggs are luminous; the grubs likewise. The adult females are magnificent lighthouses, even the adult males retain the slight glow which the grubs already possessed. We can understand the logic of the female's beacon; but of what use is all the rest of the pyrotechnic display? To my great regret, I cannot tell. It is and will continue to be, for many a day to come, perhaps for all time, a secret of animal physics, which is more mysterious than the physics of our books.

FIELD CRICKET (*Gryllus campestris*) in song.

April is coming to a close, and the song begins, single notes and discreet solos at first, but soon they break into a symphony, each clump of grass with its own performer. I would readily put the cricket at the head of the choir to herald in the spring. In the uncultivated fields of Europe, when the thyme and lavender are in flower, it has the Skylark as musical accompaniment. The lark's lyrical rising song graces the fallow land with its soft beauty, descending from the invisible bird high above. From below the cricket answers with its melody. Its song or stridulation is monotone, devoid of art, but its very simple nature is in keeping with the rustic joy of the spring revival. It is the song of the awakening, the hallelujah of the sprouting seed and the growing grass. In this duet, to whom goes the distinction? I would give it to the cricket, because it dominates by its numbers and its continuous note. Sometimes the lark keeps quiet, so that the blue-green fields of lavender, with their aromatic scent, are treated to the cricket's modest, solemn celebration.

The spring, under the full sun of midday, has the Field Cricket as its accompanist; the summer, in the calm of night, has the Tree Cricket (*Oecanthus pellucens*). One diurnal, the other nocturnal, they share the warm seasons. When the song of the first ends, the serenade of the second will soon begin.

The Tree Cricket does not share the characteristic black and heavy build of its relatives. On the contrary, it is pale, delicate, slender, almost white, suited to nocturnal habits. We would be afraid to crush it if we hold it between our fingers. It can be found on shrubs of all varieties, and on high grasses. Its life is an aerial one, and it rarely condescends to come down to the ground. It performs its night-time concerts on calm warm nights from July until October, beginning after the sun has set and continuing for a large part of the night.

BUTTERFLY-LION (*Libelloides coccajus*)
on field grass.

TREE CRICKET (*Oecanthus pellucens*) on a Love-in-a-Mist capsule.

The song is a soft and slow *gree-ee-ee, gree-ee-ee*, rendered all the more expressive by a light quaver. When we hear it, we witness the extreme subtlety of the sounds produced by its vibrating membranes. If nothing troubles the insect, sitting on the lower foliage, the sound will remain constant; but at the slightest disturbance, the performer becomes a ventriloquist. You hear it there, right in front of you, and then suddenly you hear it in the distance, some 20 feet away, continuing its couplet, muffled by the distance.

You walk towards the new sound, but find nothing. Now the sound is coming from the original location, but wait, it has changed again. This time it is coming from the left, perhaps from the right, or from behind. Complete indecision takes over – you cannot orientate youself towards the stridulating insect. A good dose of patience and meticulous attention are required to capture the performer, aided by the light of a lantern.

LILY BUSH CRICKET (*Tylopsis lilifolia*) on a Love-in-a-Mist capsule.

wasp's nest

PAPER WASP (*Polistes gallicus*) nest attached to a spurge plant.

Let's think for a moment about the beginnings of the wasp nest. It is easy with the Paper Wasp that I discovered constructing on a hedge branch. In the spring, while the nest-building is just beginning, the queen wasp works alone. Around her, there are no collaborators nor zealous competitors to put up wall against wall. She lays out the first cell. Nothing gets in her way, nothing forces her to build one form rather than another; yet the initial cell is a perfect hexagon, as the others to follow will be. It is a testament to the impeccable geometry that this insect somehow innately understands.

The wasp's nest is constructed from a thin and flexible grey paper. Textured with bands of varying shades, it reflects the nature of the wood used to build it. Arranged in simple and continuous layers, in accordance with the method of the Median Wasp (*Vespa media*), the end product would offer little protection against the cold. However, as the hot-air balloon designer knows how to preserve heat with an air bed held between several envelopes one over the other, the wasp, without studying the laws of thermodynamics, arrives at the same result by different means. From her paper paste, she manufactures large scales that loosely overlap and are stacked on top of each other in many layers. The whole forms a crude envelope, spongy, thick and full of still air. Inside such a shelter, temperatures must reach tropical levels on hot days. The same principles of spherical construction and captive air are utilised by the fierce European Hornet (*Vespa crabro*), undisputed head of the wasp order thanks to its vigour and aggressive behaviour. In the cavernous hole of a willow or in the corner of an abandoned attic, it produces a golden, streaked, flaky, cardboard-like pulp, composed of ligneous fragments bonded together. Its spherical nest is enveloped by a wall of convex scales, like tiles joined together and arranged in multiple layers, creating pockets to trap air.

PAPER WASP (*Polistes gallicus*)

crab spider

CRAB SPIDER (*Misumena vatia*)
with its prey (a domestic Honey Bee) on an Ox-eye Daisy.

Like the crab, the crab spider walks from side to side, and has stronger front limbs than back. To complete the likeness, all it needs are pinching claws on its front limbs, held ready in a boxing position.

This spider has no need for the webs that its related species spin to catch their prey. Without a net, it waits to ambush amongst the flowers. On the arrival of its prey, the spider strikes it skilfully with a single blow to the neck. This species of crab spider is particularly and passionately devoted to hunting the domestic Honey Bee. The bee arrives, peaceful and eager to gather pollen and nectar. With its proboscis, it probes the flowers, and chooses a fruitful spot from which to feed. It is soon completely absorbed in its meal. While it fills its pollen baskets and sucks up the nectar, the Crab Spider, marauder in waiting under the cover of the flowers, emerges from its hiding place, circles the prey, stealthily approaches it, and with a swift strike seizes its prey behind its head, by the neck.

CRAB SPIDER (*Misumena vatia*)
on a Ragwort flower.

BEE BEETLE (*Trichius* sp.) on a rose.

In vain the bee struggles and haphazardly strikes with its stinger, but the assailant does not loosen its grip. The bite to the nape has dealt a lethal blow to the bee's cervical ganglia. In a matter of seconds, the poor creature stretches its legs and it is over. At ease now, the assassin drinks the blood of its victim, then disdainfully discards the dried up cadaver. Once again, it waits to ambush, ready to bleed another victim if the opportunity arises. The size difference between the assailant and the assailed seems so great, given the latter's physical strength and powerful weapons, that such a fight seems impossible without the use of a net, a silk mesh to impede and restrain the formidable prey. The contrast would not be greater if the sheep dared to strike at the throat of the wolf. Nonetheless, the audacious attack does take place, and victory goes to the weaker, as is evidenced by the numerous dead bees that I watch being sucked one by one, for hours at a time by crab spiders. The relative weakness must be compensated for by a special art; the arachnid must possess a strategy that allows it to overcome this apparently insurmountable challenge.

Moving its fangs from spot to spot, as its prey is being drained, the little spider gorges on the victim's blood with a sensuous slowness. I have seen meals last seven hours long, and still the prey was only abandoned when the spider was startled by my indiscreet examination. The abandoned cadaver, an object of no value to the arachnid, is in no way dismembered. No trace of gnawed flesh, no apparent wound. The bee is drained of blood, that is all.

CRAB SPIDER (*Misumena vatia*)
hiding between the petals of a rose.

NURSERY WEB SPIDER (*Pisaura mirabilis*)
and its eggs in the heart of a rose.

FIREBUGS (*Pyrrhocoris apterus*)
on a hibiscus trunk.

EUROPEAN CICADA (*Tibicina haematodes*) attached to the trunk of a plum tree to undergo its metamorphosis.

The full-grown cicada nymph emerges from the ground where it has lived and grown for years, leaving a gaping exit hole. It roams the area in search of aerial support, a small bush, tuft of thyme, clump of grass, twig or shrub. Finding one, it climbs up and clings tightly, head up, with the claw-like ends of its front legs locked into place. The other legs, if the arrangement of the branch permits it, contribute to the balancing act; or if this is not feasible, the two hooks will suffice. Next, it rests briefly to allow the suspending arms to stiffen into immovable supports.

The mesothorax breaks first along the centreline of the back. The nymph's sides slowly crack and the soft green colour of the insect inside begins to show through. Nearly at the same

moment, the prothorax begins to crack as well. The longitudinal fissure spreads to the back of the head and along the lower mesothorax, without going any further. Across and in front of the eyes, the cranial envelope breaks, and the red eyes appear. The green parts exposed by these ruptures begin to swell and bulge out at the mesothorax. There are slow alternating palpitations caused by the inflow and outflow of blood. This swelling, invisibly at work, causes the corner to break, that will in turn break the breastplate along the two crucial lines of least resistance.

The emergence is progressing quickly. Now the head is free. The rostrum and front limbs are slowly making their way out of

their sheath. The body is horizontal, ventral side up. Under the carapace, largely open, the posterior limbs begin to appear, the last to free themselves. The wings fill with fluid. Still creased, they are tiny, thick, crumpled arcs. Ten minutes sufficed for this first phase of the transformation.

Now we move on to the second phase, longer in duration. The insect is entirely free, save the end of the abdomen, still trapped in its casing. The sloughed outer shell continues to clasp firmly to the branch. Now rigid from its prompt desiccation, it remains invariably in the position it originally held. It will form the support for what is to follow. Held back from releasing itself by the abdomen tip that remains in its casing, the cicada rotates

backwards following the vertical, its head facing down. It is a pale green, shaded yellow. The crumpled little wings now straighten up, unfurl and spread out due to the influx of liquid that fills them.

This slow and delicate operation over with, the cicada, in a nearly undetectable movement, straightens itself with its lumbar strength and reassumes its normal position, head facing upwards. The front limbs attach themselves to the empty carapace, and finally the belly is extracted from its casing. The removal is over. In all, the task took half an hour.

EUROPEAN CICADA (*Tibicina haematodes*) on the branch of a plum tree.

There stands the insect having shed its skin, but how different it is from what it will soon become! Its wings are heavy, wet, and translucent, with bright green veins. Its prothorax and mesothorax are marked with spots of brown. The rest of the body is pale green, white in places.

A long exposure to the warm air is needed to firm up and colour the frail creature. Two hours pass without any discernable change. Suspended from its moulted outer skin by its front claws, the cicada rocks at the slightest wind, still weak, still green. Finally, its colour begins to darken, slowly at first, then more quickly, and then stops, all in the span of half an hour. The frail creature I discovered hanging from a branch at nine in the morning, now takes flight, right before my very eyes, at half past noon.

EUROPEAN CICADA (*Tibicina haematodes*)
attached to the trunk of a plum tree following its metamorphosis.

Ants (*Camponotus cruentatus*) cleaning themselves.

Ants with pupae, in an ant hill.

Let's try to redeem the singers denigrated in the fable of the cicada which idly sings all summer and the ant that industriously gathers food for the winter ahead. Every summer, cicadas come to settle by the hundreds in front of my door, attracted by the greenery and two large plane trees. There, from dawn until sunset, they hammer on with their raucous symphony. With this tiresome concert, it is impossible to think; I am unable to focus on ideas. If I have not taken advantage of the morning hours, the day is lost.

The fable has no basis in the truth of these insects' lives. However, there are indeed relations between the cicada and the ant – but these relations are the opposite of what we have been told. In no circumstances would the cicada cry famine at the doors of the ant hill, promising to loyally repay everything with interest; on the contrary, it is the ant who, pressed by the food shortage, begs to the singer. Borrowing and returning are not part of the customs of the pillager, though. It takes advantage of the cicada, and brazenly robs it. Let's look into this thievery, a curious part of the story yet untold.

In the stuffy hours of a July afternoon, while the average insect, exhausted with thirst, roams in vain looking to refresh itself on the withering flowers, the cicada laughs at the general drought. With its rostrum, a fine drill-piece, it pierces a part of its inexhaustible larder. Standing, still singing, on the branch of a shrub, it bores through the firm bark to get at the sap ripened by the sun. Its sucker now plunged into the hole like a plug, it drinks peacefully, motionless, mesmerized by the charms of the syrup and its song.

Let's observe it for some time. We will perhaps witness unexpected woes. A number of thirsty creatures are lurking about; they discover the well that seeps its liquid. They run up, first showing some reserve, contenting themselves with licking the liquor that escapes. I see all manner of creatures gathering around the oozing hole – wasps, flies, earwigs, digger wasps, spider wasps, Rose Chafers. The most tenacious are the ants. I have seen them nibble on the ends of the cicada's feet; I have encountered some pulling it by the end of its wing, climbing on its back, tickling its antennae. One audacious ant, in front of my eyes, grabbed its sucker, determined to remove it. Annoyed by these tiny assailants, and at the end of its patience, the giant finally abandons the well. Reality is clearly inverted from the roles imagined in the fable. The beneficiary, taking that which the cicada needs for itself, is the ant; that industrious artisan; sharing freely with those who are suffering is the cicada. This inversion of roles will become even more marked.

After five to six weeks of jubilation, a long life for an adult insect, the singer falls from high in the tree, exhausted by life. The sun dries it out, the feet of passers-by crush the body. The ant, that pirate always in search of booty, then stumbles upon it. It cuts up the precious find, dissects it, reduces it to bits that will help to grow its stock of provisions. It is not rare to see a cicada still living but in agony, its wing still quivering in the dust, being hauled and torn apart by a squadron of ants. After witnessing this act, you're left in no doubt of the true nature of the relations between the two insects.

summer

CICADA (*Lyristes plebejus*)
having just completed its metamorphosis.

A Paper Wasp (*Polistes gallicus*) takes flight after having gathered some dead wood to build its nest.

It is perfectly calm, the sun beating down, the air is heavy, signs of a storm approaching, but conditions that are eminently favourable to the work of bees and other nectar-feeders, who seem to sense the coming rain and increase their activities to benefit from the current conditions. The bees gather pollen with enthusiasm, the drone fly travels clumsily from one flower to another. At times, this calm community, filling their bellies with sweet nectar, is interrupted by the wasp, a pillaging insect who is drawn to the prey and not the honey.

Equally bloodthirsty, but in strength rather unequal, two species share the hunt: the Common Wasp (*Vespa vulgaris*), which captures drone flies, and the European Hornet (*Vespa crabro*), which enjoys a diet of domestic Honey Bees. For both, the hunting technique is the same. In an impetuous flight, crossing over and back, the two outlaws explore the bed of flowers. When a victim is located, they abruptly dash for their coveted prey who, on its guard, flies away as the snatcher collides with the deserted flower-head in its mad dash. The chase continues in the air; not unlike a Sparrowhawk pursuing a lark. However, the bee and the drone fly, with abrupt sharp turns, have soon evaded the wasp and hornet's attacks, so they resume their roaming over the flower bed. A target less swift in its escape will be captured sooner or later. Once seized, the Common Wasp lets itself drop to the ground with its drone fly; I also lay down on the ground, slowly pulling back the dead leaves and blades of grass with my hands that could get in the way of my view. I can witness the whole drama, as long as I take care not to frighten the hunter.

Hoverfly (*Syrphus* sp.)
flying towards the stamen of a St John's Wort flower.

The Amazing Society of Bees

'In my village and far beyond it, there is a popular belief
that in order to soothe the pain of a bee or wasp sting,
all that is required is to rub the sting with three type of
herbs. Take, they say, any three different species of herbs,
the first to come up, make a bouquet of them and rub
vigorously with the infallible remedy. Initially, I thought
this a therapeutic eccentricity, as are common in rural
imaginations. However, after having tested it, I recognize
that there is some truth to its medicinal properties.
Rubbing with the three types of herbs effectively soothes
the pain of bee and wasp stings.'

Jean-Henri Fabre

Left:

HONEY BEES (*Apis mellifera*)
in a hive.

BIRTH OF A WORKER BEE (*Apis mellifera*)

Right:

HONEY BEE (*Apis mellifera*)
gathering pollen on a Sunflower.

HONEY BEE (*Apis mellifera*)
exiting a marrow flower.

SOLITARY BEE (*Dasypoda* sp.) resting on a Chicory flower.

First up we have the wasp and the larger drone fly. An untidy battle takes place in the jumble of the lawn. The fly is not armed, but it is vigorous; a sharp cry points to its desperate resistance. The wasp has its dagger; but does not know how to make best use of it, ignoring the weak areas so well known to other predators in need of fresh prey. What its young require is a soup of flies ground up to order; so to the wasp, the manner of the prey's execution is of little consequence. The stinger is used indiscriminately, blindly, with no clear method. We see it strike variously at the backside, the flanks, the head, the thorax or the stomach, following the opportunities that arise in the head to head battle. Parasitic wasps, which paralyse their victim, act as surgeons, whose able hands direct the scalpel; but this wasp attacks its prey as a crude assassin, who, in its fight, stabs randomly. The drone fly resists for an extended period, and its death is rather the result of scissor gashes than stings with the dagger. These scissors are the mandibles of the wasp, cutting, ripping open, dismembering. Once the drone fly is strangled, immobilized in the wasp's grip, the head falls with one blow of the mandibles; then the wings are cut off at their juncture with the shoulder. The legs follow, cut off one by one; finally the belly is set aside, but first emptied of its innards, which the wasp places alongside its favourite piece – the fly's thorax,

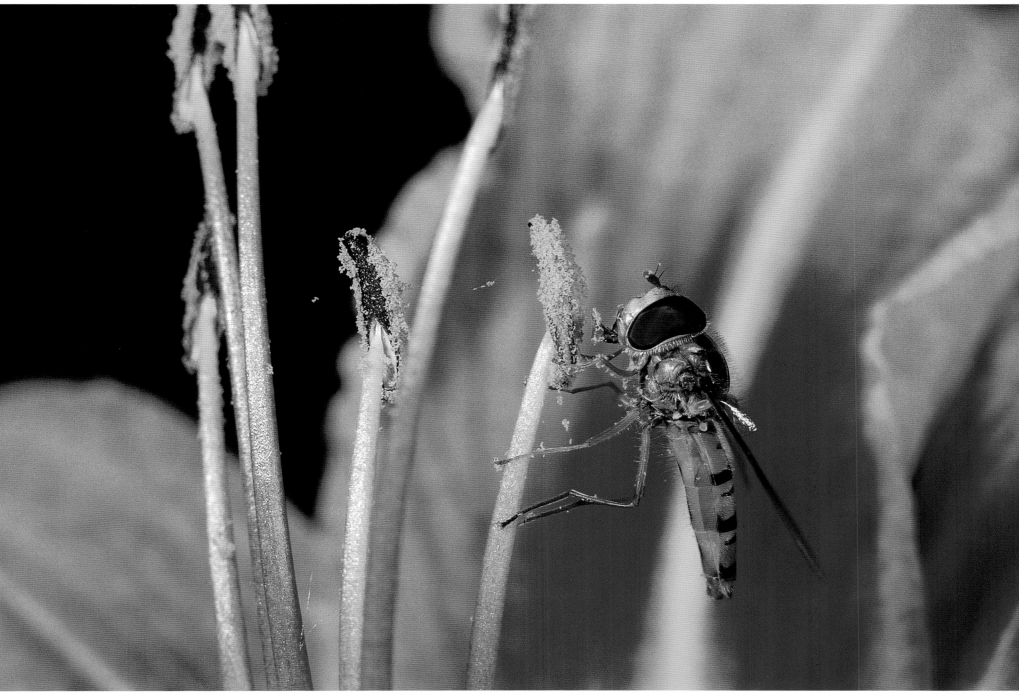

HOVERFLY (*Episyrphus balteatus*) gathering pollen on a Daylily flower.

richer in muscle than the rest of its body. Without any further delay, the wasp flies away carrying the thorax between its legs. Arriving at the nest, it will process this to feed the hungry larvae.

This is how the hornet, having just captured a Honey Bee, proceeds. In its case, the fight will not be a prolonged one, thanks to its large size and in spite of the victim's stinger. On the flower where the capture took place, or more often on the branch of a neighbouring shrub, the hornet prepares its attack. The bee's stomach is first punctured, and the honey that flows from it, lapped up. The catch is therefore a double one: a drop of honey, treat for the hunter, and the bee itself for the hornet's larvae.

Sometimes the wings are detached, as well as the abdomen; but generally the hornet contents itself with turning the bee into a shapeless mass, that it carries away without discarding anything. It is at the nest that the parts of little nutritional value, such as the wings, are discarded. Finally, it processes what's left into a form that the larvae can ingest by grinding the body between its mandibles, after having removed its wings, legs and occasionally its abdomen.

75

BRIMSTONE BUTTERFLY (*Gonepteryx rhamni*) on a Lavender flower.

ROUGH-BACKED BUSH CRICKET (*Uromenus rugosicollis*)
on a Lavender flower.

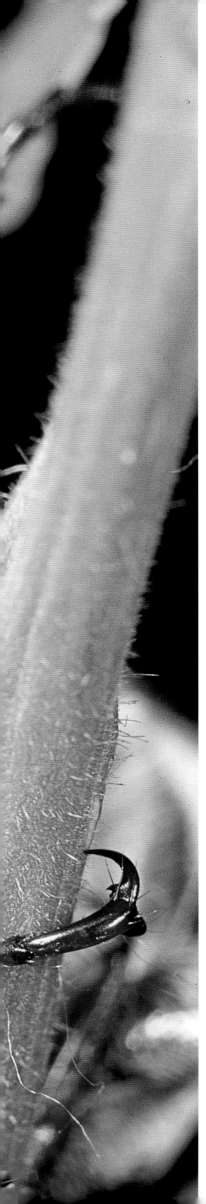

A BUTTERFLY of the Lycaenidae family sunning itself.

This pretty creature makes its appearance around the summer solstice, roughly the same time as the first cicadas. The precision of its emergence time places it firmly in the entomological calendar, no less fine tuned than that of the seasons. When the longer days arrive, those endless days that shine their golden light on the fields, it will not miss the opportunity to run up its tree. The St John's day fires, reminiscent of the sun festivals, lit by the children in the streets of the village, are no more punctual in their timing.

At this time of year, during the twilight hours, every night if the weather is calm, the insect comes to visit the pine trees in the pen. I follow its progress with a keen eye. In a silent and purposeful flight, the males circle around, spreading their feathery antennae; searching for the branches where the females are waiting for them; they pass, and pass again, their dark profiles set against the pale sky where the last light of day is waning. They stop, leave again and restart their bustling rounds. What are they doing up during the 15 nights of the festival? It is clear: they are courting the lovely females, continuing their tribute until the night comes to a close. The following morning, males and females can be found in the lower branches. They seem unaware, still, indifferent to what is happening around them. They do not flee from the hand that seizes them. Hanging from their hind legs, most of them are munching on a pine needle. Softly they doze off, the needle in their mouths. When dusk has returned, they resume their frolicking.

MALE COCKCHAFER (*Melolontha melolontha*)
at night.

79

CICADA (*Tibicina haematodes*) on a tree trunk.

In my neighbourhood, I can collect five species of cicadas that I am aware of: *Cicada plebeia*; *Cicada orni*; *Cicada hermatodes*; *Cicada atra* and *Cicada pymoea*. The first two are extremely common but the three others are rather more rare, barely known by the country folk. The most common of these is the largest and most liked, whose music is the most often described. If the weather is calm and warm, around noon, the cicada's song breaks into verses lasting a few seconds and punctuated by short silences. The verse begins abruptly. It rises quickly, the abdomen oscillating more and more quickly, achieving its greatest melodic richness. It holds the note for a few seconds, then trails off by degrees and then deteriorates into a quaver that subsides as the belly comes to a rest. Following the last abdominal beats silence intervenes, for a length of time dependant on the atmospheric conditions. Then, suddenly, a new verse begins, a monotonous repetition of the first, and so on indefinitely. Sometimes, particularly on muggy nights, the insect, intoxicated by the sun, abridges the silences or cuts them out altogether. The song is then continuous, but always alternating crescendo and decrescendo. It is towards seven or eight in the morning that the first stroke of the bow is heard, and the orchestra does not stop until the faint light of dusk fades away, around eight o'clock at night. A complete turn of the sundial marks the concert's length. However, if the sky is overcast, or if the wind is too cold, the cicada keeps quiet.

CICADAS (*Cicada orni*)
mating on a pine trunk.

cicada

MALE CICADA (*Lyristes plebejus*) singing.

Song is easier to study. I hear the first cicadas around the summer solstice. One month later, the orchestra reaches its full crescendo. A few latecomers, extremely rare, play lonely solos until the middle of September. Then, that's the end of the concert. As all do not emerge from the earth at the same time, September's lone singers are not contemporaries to those of the solstice. If we take the average between these two extremes, we come up with roughly five weeks' adult lifespan.

Four years of hard labour as a larva underground for just over a month of celebration in the sun – such is the cicada's life. Let's no longer reproach the adult cicada for its ecstatic triumph. For four years it scoured the soil in the darkness; and now the muddy earth worker is suddenly dressed in an elegant costume, bestowed with wings that rival those of birds, spoiled with heat and bathed with light, supreme joy of this world. The cicada's song will never be too noisy to celebrate bliss such as this, so well-deserved, so ephemeral.

CICADA (*Cicada orni*) blending in with its environment on a pine trunk.

SPIDER (*Argiope lobata*)
encasing a cicada.

YOUNG PRAYING MANTIS (*Mantis religiosa*) on a wild oat plant.

Yet another creature of mid-day is worthy of at least as much attention as the cicada, although it is less well-known – this is because it does not make itself heard. If it had been granted a song, it would eclipse the renown of the famous singer, so strange are its form and its behaviour. We call it the creature that prays to God. Its official name is Praying Mantis (*Mantis religiosa*).

The language of science and the simpler vocabulary of farmers are in agreement here, and equate the creature to a priestess conjuring the spirits, an ascetic in mystic ecstasy. The comparison dates from long ago. The Ancient Greeks called the insect 'mantiz', the soothsayer, the prophet. The field workers are apt at providing analogies to describe it; they fill in the vague clues given by its appearance. They saw, on the pastures dried by the sun, an insect with great presence, majestically standing ready to pounce. They noticed its full, fine green wings, woven like long linen sails; they have seen its front legs, arms so to speak, held up towards the sky in an evocative posture. Nothing more was needed; the popular imagination filled in the rest; and thus, since ancient times, the undergrowth has been populated by soothsayers conjuring oracles, by religious figures in prayer.

Oh good people of childish naivety, how mistaken you are! These higher airs hide the creature's atrocious habits; its upraised arms are those of a brigand. They do not offer prayers, but rather exterminate those who pass within their reach. Unlike other insects in the mostly herbivorous grasshopper order, the mantis feeds exclusively on living prey. It is the tiger of otherwise peaceful insect populations, the wolf in ambush that takes pleasure in fresh flesh. Its strength, vigour, carnivorous appetite and trapping skills display such horrible perfection that it should be the terror of the countryside. The apparently pious creature is in truth a satanic vampire.

YOUNG PRAYING MANTIS (*Mantis religiosa*)
with its prey, a cicada (*Cicada orni*).

87

PRAYING MANTIS (*Mantis religiosa*) on a Teasel flower.

Its instruments of death aside, the mantis has little to inspire unease. It is attractive enough with with its slender tail, its elegant bodice, its soft green colour, and its long gauze-like wings. No ferocious mandibles opening like shears; on the contrary a fine pointed snout that seems made to be used as a beak. Thanks to a flexible neck that extends far enough from the thorax, the neck can turn from right to left, tilt up, and straighten up. Unique among insects, the mantis directs its sight; it inspects, examines; it almost has facial expressions.

FEMALE PRAYING MANTIS (*Mantis religiosa*)
camouflaged amongst the grasses.

PRAYING MANTIS (*Mantis religiosa*) on a rose.

There is great contrast between the form of the body, very inoffensive in its appearance, and the murderous machines which are its front legs, designed to seize and dispatch prey. The 'thighs' of these forelegs are of unusual length and strength. Their role is to propel the trap that the victim does not see coming. Some finery also embellishes the trapper. The interior of the base of the hip has a pretty black spot circled with white; a few rows of fine pearls complete the decoration. The 'thigh', long and bobbin-shaped, has a double row of sharp spikes on the front half of its interior face. The inner row has a dozen, alternating longer black and shorter green spikes. These alternating unequal barbs contribute to the weapon's efficiency. The outer row is simpler and consists of only four teeth. Finally, three spikes, the longest of all, are located behind the two rows. Essentially, it is a saw with two parallel blades, separated by a gutter for the folded leg.

The lower part of the leg, very moveable in its articulation, is also a double saw with smaller but more numerous and tightly positioned teeth than those of the upper part. It ends in a sturdy pitchfork, whose point could rival the sharpness of the best needles with its double knife blades or hooks.

A tool of utmost perfection in piercing and tearing, this harpoon has led to many painful experiences for me. At times, in my hunt, clawed by the creature that I had just captured and not having both hands free, I have had to rely on help from others to free me from my clinging captor! Should you attempt to extricate yourself by force, without first carefully removing the embedded hooks, you will sustain scratches as painful as those from the thorns of a rose.

YOUNG PRAYING MANTIS (*Mantis religiosa*)
cleaning its feet on a Cornflower.

Latticed Heath moth caterpillar *(chiasmia clathrata)* on a bramble branch.

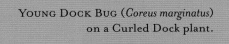

Young Dock Bug (*Coreus marginatus*) on a Curled Dock plant.

The adult Conehead Mantis is a remarkable-looking creature, even more so than the Praying Mantis. In its juvenile form it develops the pointed head, saw-like arms, long bodice and the triple row of blades on the interior face of the belly; but the belly does not yet curve into a full arch, and the animal has a more normal shape. In adulthood large, soft green wings, pink near the joints, overlay a white and green striped pattern on the abdomen. The male, which is the more striking of the sexes, sports feathery antennae, similar to those of the silk moths of the family Bombycidae. A few small structural details aside, the Conehead Mantis is identical to the Praying Mantis. In terms of size, it is nearly as large as its relative. The farmer mistakes it for the other. When, in the spring, he encounters the young Conehead Mantis, he thinks it to be its more famous cousin. Similar morphology would suggest

similar habits and customs. Judging by its extravagant armour, it would be tempting to ascribe a more violent nature to the Conehead Mantis than that of the Praying Mantis. This was my first inclination, and it's easy to see why others would think the same, confident in this fallacious analogy. Time to disperse these myths: despite its ferocious appearance, the Conehead Mantis is a gentler creature.

The voracious Praying Mantis is short-tempered. Its stomach filled with crickets, the Praying Mantis is easily irritated and assumes its boxing pose. The Conehead Mantis, frugal in its eating habits, does not indulge in such hostile displays. Not one to quarrel, it never spreads open its wings in a threatening display, unlike its cousin; nor does it express the vaguest desire to engage in the Praying Mantis's cannibalistic feasts. These horrors are completely unknown to it.

Young Conehead Mantis (*Empusa pennata*) on an Eryngo leaf.

I do not know of a more touching love story than that of the Conehead Mantis. The male is devoted, enterprising, and faces a long ordeal before achieving success. For days and days, he pesters the female, who eventually gives in. All is well after the wedding party. The male mantis withdraws, unmolested by the female who keeps busy with her hunting and shows no sign of turning on her partner.

The two sexes then cohabitate in peace, indifferent to one another, until the middle of July. At this point, the male, worn out by time, ceases to hunt and shows signs of exhaustion, staggering about and slowly descending from the heights of the vegetation to collapse on the ground. Thus it meets its end. The male Praying Mantis, let's not forget, becomes a meal for the female as soon as they have mated.

The females lay their eggs not long after the deaths of the males. About to build its nest, the female Conehead Mantis does not develop the enlarged stomach of a female Praying Mantis, weighed down by her many eggs. Always svelte and lightweight, the Conehead produces only a small number of eggs.

How can we account for these profound differences between these two very similar species? From the diet perhaps? Why then, is one prone to overeating, the other to reticence, when their nearly identical build would seem to have arisen to fulfil these needs? The mantises demonstrate to us what we have already heard before: the details of behaviour are not under the exclusive domain of anatomy. Above the laws of physics that govern matter, there are other laws which govern instinct.

Ladybird

SEVEN-SPOT LADYBIRD (*Coccinella septempunctata*) feeding on Rose Aphids (*Macrosiphum rosae*).

et's now turn to the elegant tribe of the ladybirds. The most common is the Seven-spot Ladybird, adorned with its red carapace and seven distinguishing black spots. It is known in France as 'God's animal', a creature of great renown. Young village girls place it on an extended finger, let it go and sing to it:

> *Digo-me, Catarineto,*
> *Ounte passarai*
> *Quand me maridarai.*
> *(Tell me, Ladybird,*
> *What will happen*
> *When I marry.)*

The ladybird decisively takes flight. If it flies towards the church, destiny is the convent; in the other direction, it means marriage. This myth is based perhaps on ancient beliefs relating to the flight of birds.

It is unfortunate that the insect's gentle reputation should be in conflict with its behaviour. Here, as ever, reality destroys the poetry. In truth, 'God's animal' is involved in carnage, a slaughterer in the highest degree, whose ferocity is unmatched. It slowly grazes colonies of aphids, leaving none behind. Where it feeds with its equally carnivorous larva, no living thing remains on the stems.

Ant and its colony of aphids on
a poppy stem.

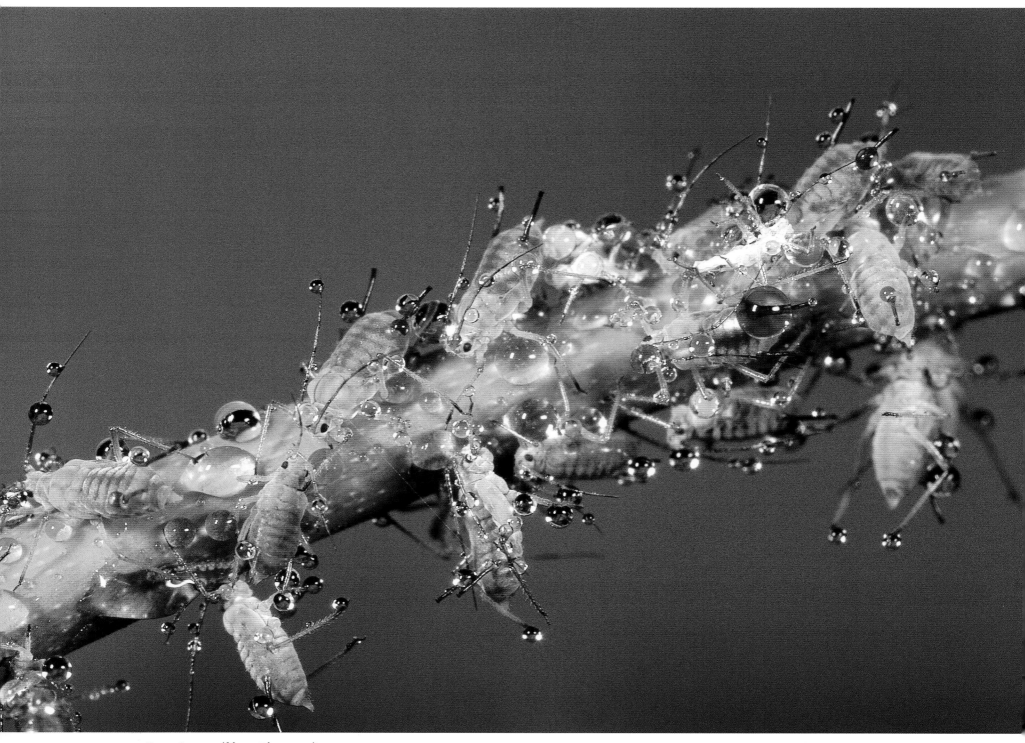

If the summer becomes a little cool, the broom shrubs are soon busy with innumerable black aphids who, packed next to one another, cover the green branches with an animal bark. As other insects have discovered, these tiny bugs have, near the bottom of their bellies, two deep cornicula or tubes of syrup, the ant's favourite sweet.

They are the ant's cows. The ants come to milk them, or rather provoke them by tickling to discharge the sweet liquor. As soon as it appears at the end of the tubes, the drop is lapped up by its milkman. There are some ants with more elaborate aspirations, that corral a herd of aphids in a pen built of earth around a tuft of greenery. Without leaving their homes, the ants can milk and fill their stomachs. I have discovered many a tuft of thyme at the foot of my broom shrubs that has been converted in this way. However, numerous and enthusiastic though they may be, these milkmen cannot consume all of the products of such a herd. The sacs begin to expel the excess liquid and let it fall carelessly. The branches and leaves beneath receive the exquisite dew and are

SEVEN-SPOT LADYBIRD (*Coccinella septempunctata*) larva devouring aphids on a rose stem.

glazed by a viscous coating, the honeydew. This caramel, cooked by the sun, draws masses of gourmets that are not versed in the art of milking: wasps, ladybirds, chafers, flies and midges primarily, of all sizes and colours. This innumerable mass, buzzing and swarming, suck, lick, and rake up the honeydew. The aphid is the official sweet-maker of the insect world; it generously invites all the thirsty insects of the blistering summer months to share its confectionery.

great green Bush cricket

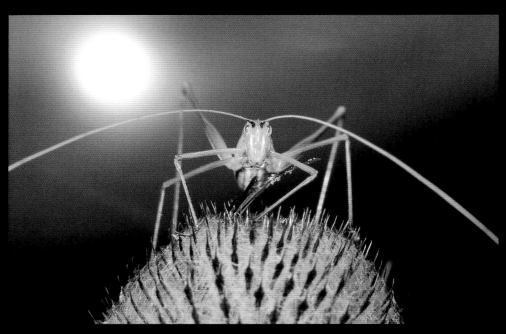

YOUNG GRASSHOPPER in the subfamily Phaneropterinae on a woolly thistle.

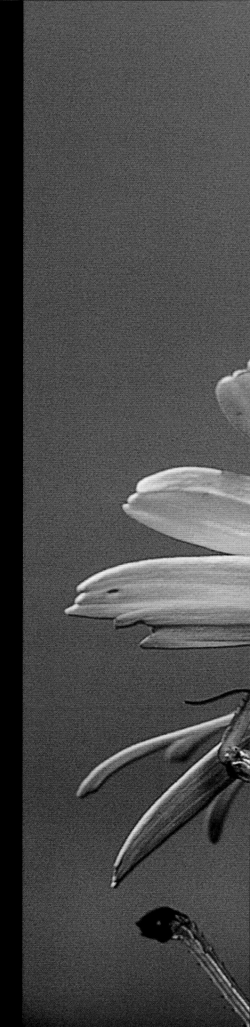

I t's late, and the cicadas have quieted. Satiated by the light and the heat, they lavished us with their symphonies all day. Now that night has fallen, they try to rest. This rest, however, is a troubled one. In the thick, leafy branches of the plane tree, a sudden noise, like a shriek of anxiety, piercing and short, is heard. It is the desperate cry of a cicada, surprised out of its sleep by a Great Green Bush Cricket, that fervent nocturnal hunter, that pounced on it, to trap it and open up its belly to delve inside. The musical prelude is followed by carnage.

At dawn, I was a hundred steps away from my door when something fell from the neighbouring plane tree with a sharp squeak. I ran up to it. It was a cricket emptying the belly of a cicada, showing no restraint. The cicada whirred and struggled in vain – the grasshopper did not loosen its grip, plunging its head deep into the cicada's entrails and removing them in small mouthfuls.

I had been alerted to the attack that took place up there, while the cicada was resting. The struggles of the unfortunate victim, being dissected alive, had caused the predator and its prey to drop together from the tree. Later, on numerous occasions, I have had the opportunity to witness many more such massacres.

GREAT GREEN BUSH CRICKET (*Tettigonia viridissima*) on a Teasel leaf.

I have seen a Great Green Bush Cricket jump boldy in pursuit of a cicada which had fled in a frantic flight, not unlike the Sparrowhawk in pursuit of the lark up in the sky. The hunter in this case is the smaller and weaker insect. The cricket attacks a heavyweight, who is much larger and much stronger than its opponent; but nonetheless the result of this disproportionate wrestling match is never in doubt. With its strong jaws and sharp claws, the cricket rarely fails to rip open its captive who, with no weapons to defend itself, can only cry and wriggle about. The key is to hold it in place, which is easier during the drowsiness of night. All cicadas that encounter the fierce cricket during the nocturnal hours will surely perish pitifully. This explains the sudden squeaking sounds of anguish that come from the leafy branches during the late hours of the night – they are startling, as the cicadas' song has long since ended. The bandit, dressed in celadon green, has caught a sleeping cicada.

GREAT GREEN BUSH CRICKET (*Tettigonia viridissima*)

Feeding on sweet cicadas is not possible in all countries. In northern countries, where cicadas are less abundant or absent, the cricket will not find the prey that it so cherishes. It must search for other food.

These examples teach us enough. They tell us that the cricket is a fervent consumer of insects, particularly those that are not protected by a hard carapace; they confirm its highly carnivorous tastes, though it is not exclusively a flesh-eater, unlike the related Praying Mantis who refuses everything but live prey. The executioner of cicadas is happy to supplement its diet with plant material as well. After the flesh and blood, it enjoys sweet pulp of fruit and, for lack of a better alternative, sometimes even a little greenery.

LILY BUSH CRICKET (*Tylopsis lilifolia*)
at sunset.

Rough-backed Bush Cricket (*Uromenus rugosicollis*)
on a Teasel flower.

A Digger Wasp dragging a large Great Green Bush Cricket (*Tettigonia viridissima*).

Fortune has its entomological whims: you run after it, and can't find it; you forget about it, but then here it is knocking at your door. What a futile chase I have had to see the Digger Wasp capture its cricket prey, what a pointless preoccupation this has been! Twenty years have passed since I first tried. These pages were already with the printer when in the early days of this month (8 August 1878), my son Émile rushed into my office. 'Quickly,' he said, 'come quickly, a Digger Wasp is dragging its prey under the plane trees, in front of the door in the yard.' Knowing about the wasp's habit from bedtime stories and details garnered from our life in the fields, I knew Émile's description was accurate. I ran up to see a superb Digger Wasp dragging a paralyzed cricket by its antennae. It was heading towards the neighbouring chicken coop, and seemed to want to scale the wall, to establish its den up above, under some roof tiles. I had seen a similar Digger Wasp make the same climb with its prey a few years earlier, and elect to take up residence under the shelter of

dislodged tiles. A similar process was now repeating itself, and this time in front of numerous witnesses, for the entire household has gathered in the shade of the plane trees to encircle the Digger Wasp. We admired the sheer audacity of the insect, whose attention was not diverted by the gallery of curious onlookers. We were all struck by its proud and robust air, as it dragged the enormous burden behind it, its victim's antennae in its mandibles, its head high. Alone amongst the audience, I experienced regret at this spectacle. 'If only I had some live crickets!' I couldn't help myself from saying, without the smallest hope to have my wish fulfilled. Émile said, 'Live crickets? I have some that I gathered this morning.' He took the stairs four at a time, and ran up to his little study, where the walls of dictionaries act as an educational playground for a few pretty Spurge Hawkmoth caterpillars. He brought me back three crickets, better than I could have hoped, two females and a male.

Large Conehead (*Ruspolia nitidula*) attached to a blade of grass.

digger wasp

COMMON HOLLYHOCKS.

How did these insects appear at my disposal, at that precise moment when I needed them? This is another story. A Southern Grey Shrike had built its nest high on the plane tree along the path. A few days before, the mistral, brutal wind of this region, blew so violently that the branches swayed as well as the grasses. The nest was flipped over by the swaying of its support, and the four nestlings that it held had fallen out. The following morning, I found the nest on the ground. Three had died from the fall, the fourth was still alive. I entrusted the survivor's care to Émile and he went on the hunt for crickets in the neighbourhood lawns three times a day to feed the nestling. However, the crickets were small, and the appetite of the infant bird demanded large numbers of them. There was another, more substantial option – the bush cricket, and these were gathered as a provision from time to time, among the thatch and prickly foliage of sea holly. The three bush crickets Émile brought to me came from the shrike's pantry. My sympathy for the homeless nestling owed me this undreamed of success.

The circle of spectators enlarged to allow the Digger Wasp free passage. I removed its prey with pliers and quickly passed it one of the living bush crickets in exchange, a female armed with a sabre at the end of its belly just like the prey I'd taken away. A few stamps of its feet were the only signs of annoyance displayed by the deprived wasp. It then ran up to its new prey, which was too corpulent to even attempt to escape. The wasp grabbed hold of the cricket's thorax with its mandibles, and using it like a saddle, placed itself across it. Curling its abdomen, it moved its stinger towards the underside of the insect's thorax. Here, without a doubt, the stings were delivered, without my being able to discern the exact number because of the difficulty in observing it. The bush cricket, soon anaesthetised, allowed the operation to take place without resisting; it was the dumb sheep at the slaughterhouse. The Digger Wasp took its time, and manoeuvred its stinger with a slowness that allowed it to precisely aim its strikes. Until now, all had been clear to the observers, but the prey touched the ground with its chest and belly, and what exactly was happening beneath remained a mystery. Any thoughts of intervening to gently lift the bush cricket and get a better view were suppressed.

YOUNG BUSH CRICKET of the Phaneropterinae family feeding on the pollen of a Hollyhock flower.

Spotted Longhorn (*Rutpela maculata*) on a bramble flower.

Common Carder Bee (*Bombus pascuorum*) gathering pollen on a thistle.

The killer now sheathed its weapon and drew back. The next stage was easily observed. After having stabbed the thorax, the end of the Digger Wasp's abdomen moved under the neck, which the wasp opened by pressing against its victim's nape. Here, the stinger searched with marked persistence, as if the sting was to be more efficient here than elsewhere. One would be inclined to think that the nerve centre is located in the inferior portion of the oesophageal collar; but the continuing movement of the cricket's mouthparts, mandibles, jaws and palpus, brought to life by this innervation, showed that this is not the case. By way of the neck, the Digger Wasp reached only the thoracic ganglions, or at least the first of these, more accessible through the neck's thin skin than the teguments of the breast.

And it was over. Without any twitch or display of pain, the bush cricket was rendered into an inert mass. For the second time, I removed the lifeless victim from the Digger Wasp, and replaced it with the second female cricket at my disposal. The very same manoeuvres began again, followed by the same result. Three times in row, in rapid succession, with its own prey first, and then with the two from my exchanges, the Digger Wasp restarted its skilful surgery. Would it undertake it again a fourth time with the male bush cricket that remains? It was doubtful,

not because the wasp was weary, but because this prey is not to its liking. I have never seen it with prey other than the females, who, packed with eggs, are the wasp larvae's favourite food. My suspicion was well founded; deprived of its third captive, the Digger Wasp obstinately refused the male cricket that I presented to it. It ran hither and thither, in a mad rush, looking for its lost prey; three or four times, it neared the male bush cricket, circled it, gave it a disdainful look, and finally flew away. The male was not what its larvae needs; experience reiterates this to me in 20-year intervals.

Yet another remark: fresh meat is the de rigueur food for larvae of these wasps. If the prey was stored intact in the nest, in four or five days it would be a decaying; and the larvae, having just hatched, would only find a spoiled mass. However, stung by the wasp's needle, the prey remains alive and paralysed for two or three weeks, more than enough time for the hatching of the eggs and the larvae's development. The paralysis thus has a double result: immobilize the food, so as not to compromise the delicate larvae's survival, and ensure a long preservation of the flesh to ensure that the larva has healthy food. Enlightened by science, the logic of man could not find better.

Rough-backed Bush Cricket (*Uromenus rugosicollis*)
on a knapweed flower.

silkmoth

OAK HAWKMOTH (*Marumba quercus*) taking flight.

It is a pretty cocoon, oblong in form, recalling the products of silk culture – firm in consistency and tawny-coloured. Some brief details gleaned from books nearly confirm the Oak Eggar moth. If that was it, what a godsend! I can continue my study, perhaps complete that which made me search out the moth. These wonders were known to me through my readings; but to see, with one's own eyes, and experiment a little at the same time, is something else.

The male's costume is a monastic robe in a humble red-brown. But in this case, the frock is made of luxurious velvet, with a pale cross-stripe and a small eye-like white speck on the front wings.

Portrait of a
GYPSY MOTH CATERPILLAR (*Porthetria dispar*).

man's footprint on the planet

'Are we in a position to coexist with our own power? If the answer is no, evolution will continue without us. Like Sisyphus, we would have pushed our stone to the peak of the mountain to let it go. A little silly, is it not? We must not turn a blind eye to the gravity of the present situation. Nonetheless, it is important to remain optimistic. We must put everything in motion to save our planet before it is too late. We are responsible for it, we are its heirs. It is up to us to ensure that the beautiful history of the world continues.'

Hubert Reeves

CRUSHED INSECTS (FROM LEFT TO RIGHT):
cricket, wasp and cricket, Adonis Blue butterfly and ladybird.

scorpion

COMMON SCORPION (*Buthus occitanus*) and its young.

The objects found beneath the mother appear to be eggs, identical in every way to those you would find through dissection of the ovaries at an advanced stage of gestation. The creature inside each egg, condensed into a space-saving grain of rice, has its tail glued along its stomach, its claws tucked against its chest, its legs tightly folded, in such a way that the little oval mass does not show the slightest protuberance. On the brow, two black dots indicate eyes. The creature floats in a drop of hyaline, which is its world, its atmosphere for the moment, delineated by an extremely delicate film. Are these objects really eggs? There were, at the beginning, thirty or forty in the Common Scorpion's clutch, a little fewer than in that of the Black Scorpion. I arrived too late for the nocturnal laying, I am witnessing the end of it. The little that remains suffices to confirm my beliefs. The scorpion is in fact oviparous; but its eggs hatch very quickly, and the young's hatching quickly follows the laying.

How does this liberation occur? I have the privilege to witness it myself. I see the mother who, with the ends of her mandibles, delicately clasps, slashes, removes and swallows the egg's membrane. She lays each newborn bare with the meticulous care and tenderness of the sheep and cat when they eat the birth sac. There are no wounds on the baby scorpions' newly-formed flesh, no injury, in spite of the crudeness of the tool of choice. I can't get over my surprise. The scorpion has conducted an act of a maternity as tender as any of our own. Here are the young, meticulously removed from their eggs, clean and free. They are white. Their length, from the forehead to the end of the tail measures 9 mm for the Common Scorpion and 4 mm for the Black Scorpion. As the young are liberated they climb, one, then the next, onto the mother's back, heaving themselves up in no great hurry along the claws that the mother scorpion keeps on the ground in order to facilitate the climbing. Tightly grouped together one against the other, mixed together randomly, they form a continuous layer on the mother's back. Thanks to their small claws, they are able to stay in place.

BLACK SCORPION (*Euscorpius flavicaudis*)
on a stone.

STICK INSECT (*Clonopsis gallica*) under a rose.

The tiny youngsters are now subjected to a challenging ordeal; they must be reborn, shall we say. They prepare for this by remaining immobile, preparing to shed their skins – which is in many ways analogous to the transformation of insects from larval to adult form. In spite of their scorpion-like shape, the young have indistinct features, as if seen through the mist. It is as if they were wearing a sort of shapeless gown that they have to remove in order to become slender and gain a more distinct appearance. Eight motionless days on the mother's back are necessary to accomplish this feat. Then the skin begins to break in what I would hesitate to call sloughing, so different it is from an actual slough, that will occur later in its life on several occasions. In the latter case, the skin breaks on the thorax, and through this fissure the animal emerges leaving its old dried exoskeleton behind. The empty mould maintains the exact shape of the creature it contained.

However, for the first moult it is a completely different story. I put a few young ready to break through on a glass slide. They are not moving, but suffering it seems, almost faltering. The skin breaks without any specific lines of fracture; it rips itself from the front, back and sides at the same time; the legs are removed from their casings, the claws leave their gloves behind, the tail comes out of its sheath. From all parts the skin is falling in tatters. It is a sloughing without order and by bits. Soon the task is complete, the young take on the normal appearance of scorpions, and have also acquired their agility. Still pale in colour, they are alert, quick to come down to the ground to play and run alongside their mother. The most striking thing about this progression is the sudden growth. The young of the Common Scorpion measured 9 mm in length, and they now measure 14 mm. Those of its black cousin have gone from 4 mm to 6 or 7 mm. The length increases by half, which roughly triples their volume.

Surprised by this sudden growth, we ask ourselves how it occurs, as these little ones have not had any food. Their weight has not increased; on the contrary, it has diminished, thanks to the sloughing of the outer skin. The volume grows, but not the mass. What we have here then is a dilation, comparable to that

THICK-LEGGED FLOWER BEETLE (Œdemera nobilis) on a bramble flower.

which occurs in bodies exposed to heat. An internal change occurs, that groups the living molecules into a more spacious configuration, and the volume increases without bringing in new matter. The colour is beginning to appear; the belly and the tail take on the colour of the first light of day, the claws develop a translucent amber lustre. Youth makes everything more attractive. They are in truth magnificent creatures to behold, these scorpions. If they remained like this, if their future was not one of menacing distillers of venom, they would be graceful creatures that we would take pleasure in rearing. Soon a vague desire for emancipation will awaken in them. Willingly they descend from the maternal back to romp happily around the neighbourhood. If they spread out too far, the mother chastens them, bringing them back together with the rake of her arms.

In moments of rest, the spectacle of the scorpion and her young is nearly as impressive as that of the hen and her chicks at rest. Most of them are on the ground, tightly pushed up against their mother; a few of them crawl onto the white pillow. There are some that climb the maternal tail, and clamber high up on the

tip, and from this culminating point, seem to take pleasure in observing the crowd. New acrobats arrive to evict and succeed them. Each of them wants their share of the curiosity which is the panoramic tower.

Most of the family stays around the mother; there is continuous movement of rambling children that slip in and out from under her belly and huddle around her, their brows with their tiny sparkling black eyes pointing outwards. The more energetic ones prefer the mother's legs, which are used as gym equipment, engaging in trapeze-like acrobatics. Then, at leisure, the pack climbs on her back, take their places, and stabilize themselves until nothing is moving, not the mother or her young. This period of maturation and preparation for liberation lasts a week, as does the period leading up to the tripling of volume, free of food. In all, the family spends roughly 15 days on the mother's back.

what if only insects remained?

'It is foreseeable that the human species could die out, without life disappearing completely. Insects and their relatives, for example, are much more resistant than we are. Scorpions can survive in levels of radioactivity much higher than it would take to kill us. They could survive a nuclear war, develop their intelligence and rediscover technology. They would potentially face, in a few tens of millions of years, problems of pollution analogous to our own.'

Hubert Reeves

Left to right:

YOUNG BUSH CRICKET of the family Phaneropterinae on a rose petal.

pond

Meadow near the water.

A source of delight in my youth, the pond still provides a spectacle that my advanced years cannot grow tired of. What hustle and bustle we find in this verdant world of green algae! In small black legions, in the lukewarm mud of the edges of the pond, the little toad tadpole rests and wags its tail. Between the waters, the orange-bellied newt idly navigates with the large oar which is its flattened tail. Amongst the bulrushes are the floating caddisfly larvae, half sticking out of their cases made of small bundles of sticks, they form turrets of small shells. The diving beetle plunges into the depths of the pool, equipped with its respiratory reserves: air bubbles at the end of the wing cases, and under the chest, a thin gaseous layer that sparkles like a silver breastplate. Next to this are the unsinkable gathering of pond skaters, who slide by transverse leg movements, similar to those of the cobbler stitching his work.

Here are the water boatmen, that swim on their backs with two paddles outstretched like a cross, and the flattened water scorpions. Cloaked in mud, the nymph of the largest of our dragonflies moves forwards in a most curious way: it fills its large funnel-shaped hindquarters with water, expulses it, and continues in this way by the propulsion of its hydraulic instrument.

PAIR OF MATING DAMSELFLIES
of the Coenagrionidae family.

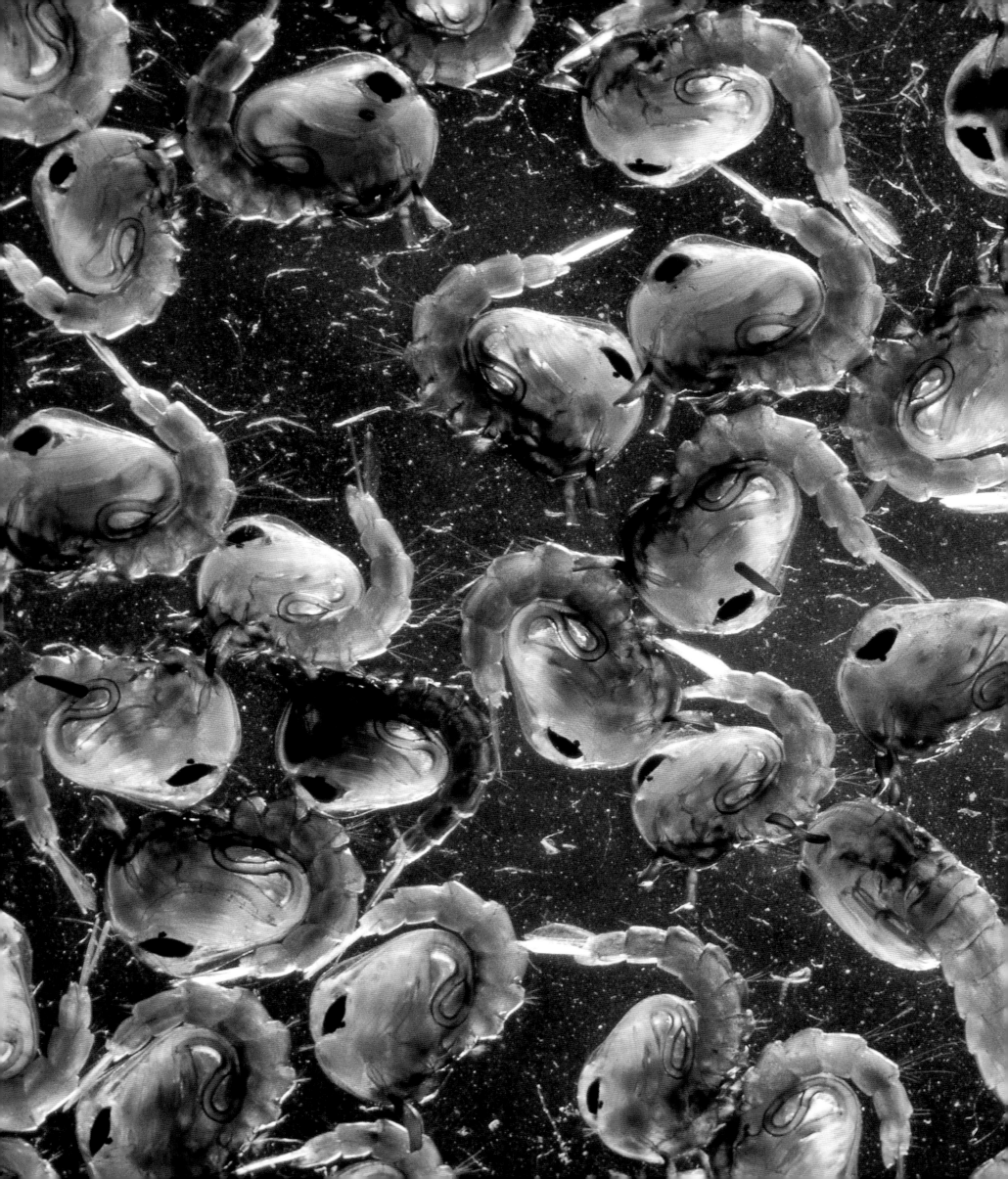

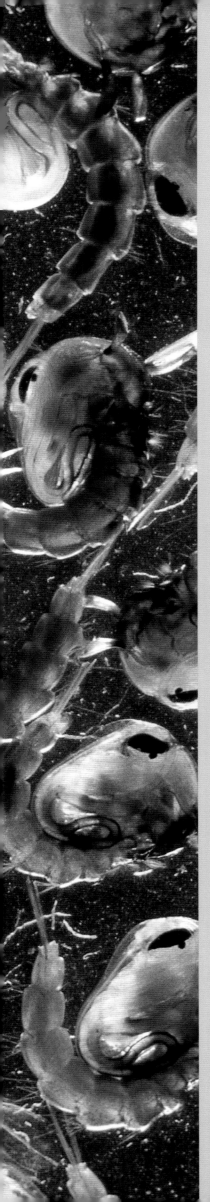

Southern Hawker dragonfly larva (*Aeshna cyanea*)
sloughing off its skin under water.

Mosquito undergoing its metamorphosis on the surface
of the water.

Mosquito chrysalises
under water.

DEMOISELLE DAMSELFLY (*Calopteryx* sp.)
against the rising sun.

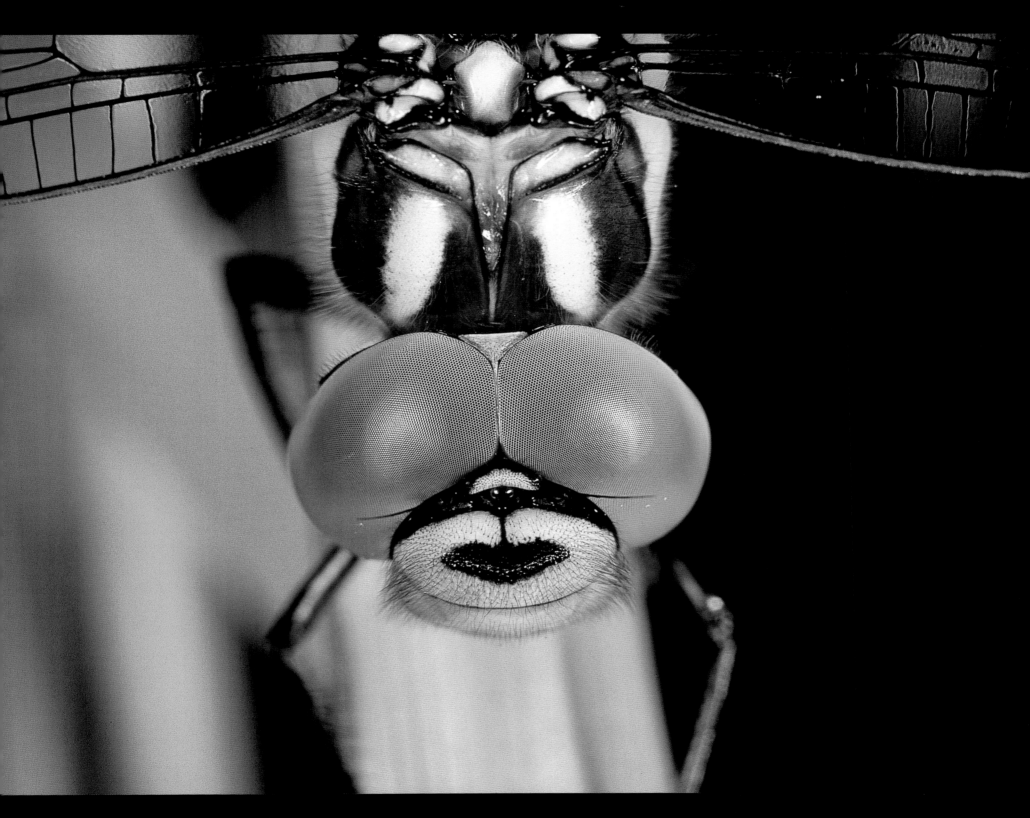

SOUTHERN HAWKER (*Aeshna cyanea*)
has huge eyes in proportion to its head.

COMMON CARDER BEE
in the centre of a Morning Glory flower.

SHIELDBUG (*Codophila* sp.)
on a scabious flower.

life of a scabious

'Why so much consistency in the curves of the flower's petals, so much elegance in the carving of the wings of a scabious? When we want to investigate more subtle details of life, questions arise that scientific investigation cannot answer. The enigma which is the world can certainly find interpretation outside of the small truths of our laboratories.'

Jean-Henri Fabre

PRAYING MANTIS (*Mantis religiosa*) on a wild carrot flower.

Its body completely still in its strange pose, the mantis watches the cricket, its vision focused in the prey's direction, its head pivoting slightly as it follows the other's every movement. The goal of this scrutiny is clear: the mantis wants to unnerve it, paralyse the powerful cricket with fear, to render it less dangerous. Does it succeed? Behind the cricket's shiny head and its long face, it is unaware of what is about to occur. No sign of emotion is revealed as we look on at their stone-faced masks. It is certain, however, that the menaced knows of the danger. It sees a spectre towering in front of it, pitchforks in the air, ready to come down on it; it feels as though it is about to face death and does not flee whilst there is still time. The great leaping insect, who could so easily soar far away from the claws, the jumper with its powerful legs, stupidly remains in place or even slowly moves towards the danger.

It is said that small birds, paralysed with terror in front of the snake's open mouth, dumbfounded by the reptile's gaze, are incapable of flight and allow themselves to be captured. The cricket often behaves in the same way. It is now within the grasp of the charmer. The two arms beat down on it, the claws harpoon, the double saws close up and clasp its prey. In vain the cricket protests: its mandibles bite at the empty air, its hind legs buck desperately in the air. The inevitable will come to pass. The mantis folds back its wings, its battle flag of choice, and reassumes its normal pose as the meal begins.

MALE PRAYING MANTIS (*Mantis religiosa*) with its prey (bush cricket) under the shade of a wild carrot flower.

mantis's prey

YOUNG PRAYING MANTIS (*Mantis religiosa*) with its prey (cricket).

In a moment of hunger, after a few days of fasting, the cricket, equal in size or larger than the Praying Mantis, is consumed in its entirety, save the wings, which are too dry for its tastes. To eat the monstrous meal, two hours will suffice. Such binging is rare. I have observed it once or twice, each time wondering how the gluttonous beast finds the space for so much food, and how the balance tips in favour of the relatively smaller predator. I admire the impressive qualities of its stomach, where food passes to be quickly digested and dissolved.

YOUNG PRAYING MANTIS (*Mantis religiosa*)
and its prey (bush cricket).

Praying Mantis (*Mantis religiosa*) devouring a bush cricket.

Green shieldbug of the family Pentatomidae
on a thistle bud.

PRAYING MANTIS (*Mantis religiosa*) in its intimidating spectral pose.

PRAYING MANTIS (*Mantis religiosa*)
cleaning its feet after a meal.

SWALLOWTAIL BUTTERFFLY (*Papilio machaon*)
at sunset, 'magnificent gossamer-winged butterfly, with its
orange eye-spots and blue crescents.'

SWALLOWTAIL CATERPILLAR (*Papilio machaon*)
under a wild carrot flower head.

metamorphosis

I have just witnessed something very moving: the last metamorphosis of a bush cricket, the adult's birth from the nymph's sheath. It is magnificent. My subject is a large Rough-legged Bush Cricket, the colossus of its kind, frequently found on the vines in September around harvest time. By its size, which can reach the length of a finger, it lends itself to observation more than others.

The first step is to burst through the old skin. Behind this, under the pointed roof of the prothorax, there are pulsations resulting from the alternating swelling and contraction. Similar efforts are going on in front of the nape, and most likely under the entire cover of the soon-to-be broken carapace. The thinness of the membranes at the joints makes it noticeable in these exposed areas, but the breastplate hides it from our eyes in the central portions of its body. The blood reserves of the creature flood in, in waves. Their rising tide creates a sort of hydraulic ram. Weakened by this pushing of fluids, in a concentrated effort by the organism, the skin finally breaks, following the path of least resistance prepared by the clever construction of life. The ripping spreads all the way along and opens precisely at the hull, a sort of soldering of two symmetrical halves. Otherwise impregnable, the envelope breaks at this median point, which has remained weaker than the rest. The slit extends a bit towards the back and descends between the anchors of the wings; it climbs back up towards the head, up to the base of the antennae, where it briefly splits. With this gap, the back begins to show, all soft, pale, faintly ash-coloured. Slowly it swells, growing a larger hump with time, and before we know it, it is completely unsheathed.

WASP SPIDER (*Argiope bruennichi*)
having completed its final moult, attached to a wild carrot.

142

metamorphosis

Female Conehead Mantis (*Empusa pennata*) on a Love-in-the-mist capsule.

The head follows, pulled out from its mask, which stays in place, intact in its finest details, but with the strange appearance of large glass eyes that are no longer looking at you. The antennae casings, unwrinkled and in their natural position, hang from the empty translucent face.

To emerge from their narrow sheath, tightly enclosed within, the antennae gave no resistance on the way out to cause their envelopes to flip inside out, deform or wrinkle in the least. Their contents, equal in size, and knobby as well, manage to free themselves as easily as a smooth object sliding out of a loosely fitting container. The mechanism of extraction will become more striking when it comes to the hind legs.

Now we move onto the front and middle legs to emerge from their casings. Yet again, without tearing a single one, without a crease in their fabric, the leg sheathes remain perfectly in their natural position. The insect is now attached only by its long hind legs. It leans vertically, head down, oscillating like a pendulum. Four small hooks provide its support in suspension. If they give way, if they were to undo, the insect would be lost, incapable of spreading its large wings anywhere but in the space. They will stay firmly in place: instinct has caused them to tighten up and strengthened before their withdrawal, so as to unshakably support the wrenching that will follow.

Praying Mantis (*Mantis religiosa*)
undergoing its final metamorphosis.

ROUGH-BACKED BUSH CRICKET (*Uromenus rugosicollis*) feeding on a Star Thistle.

Now the wings emerge. They look like four narrow rags, with faint grooves in them, like bits of fine cord in paper mâché. They are barely a quarter of their full length; so soft and pliable that they bend under the weight and fall along the insect's sides in the opposite direction that they would normally. The ends of the wings, which should be pointing towards the back, are now pointing towards the animal's head, suspended backwards. Four heavy leaves on a tree, bruised and sodden from the rain of a storm, would paint an accurate picture of the pitiful bouquet that is to become the flying organs.

ROUGH-BACKED BUSH CRICKET (*Uromenus rugosicollis*)
undergoing its metamorphosis.

CRICKET blending in with surroundings stones.

A fundamental effort must be made in order to achieve perfection of form. The internal work has already largely begun with the solidifying of the internal fluids, creating order from the shapeless mass; but nothing on the exterior would hint at what is happening in this mysterious laboratory. Everything seems inert.

While waiting, the hind legs free themselves. The large thighs are visible, their interior skin tinted a pale pink which will soon become a vivid crimson. Towards the head, hidden by the sheath, the leg is softer and in a state of the extreme plasticity, even fluidity, that allows it to navigate the difficult pathways of the sheath. I witness not only a simple discharge of the veil-like, armoured sheaths that adorn the tibias, but a sort of birth that takes one aback by its abruptness.

Finally the lower legs are freed. They fold onto themselves limply in the groove of the thigh to develop in stillness. The belly frees itself. The fine tunic begins to wrinkle, as it creases and draws towards the end that is still, for some time, involved in the process. The cricket is entirely naked excepting this one area. It hangs vertically, head facing downwards, held in place by the small claws of its now empty foot casings. Throughout this work, so meticulous and long, the four hooks have not given out, a testament to the delicacy of the insect's extraction. The cricket remains still, attached at the back by its rags. Its belly is rounded beyond measure, stretched no doubt by the accumulated fluids that will soon go towards expanding the wings. The cricket rests; it is getting over its tiredness. Twenty minutes pass.

Then, with an effort starting with its back, the hanging insect straightens up and its front feet seize the sheath attached above it. Never has an acrobat, suspended from the bar by his feet, displayed a comparable show of strength from the waist to straighten himself. This tour de force accomplished, the rest is nothing. With the leverage of the support that it has just obtained, the insect climbs up the twigs of the shrub on which it undertakes its transformation. It grabs hold with its four front legs. The end of the belly has just been liberated; and with it, the sheath, weakened by a final jolt, falls to the ground.

TREE CRICKET (*Oecanthus pellucens*)
having just finished its metamorphosis, attached to a Cornflower bud.

PAPER WASPS (*Polistes* sp.) on their nest.

The inside of the nest is taken up by disk-like layers, arranged horizontally and joined to one another by solid pillars. Their numbers are variable. Towards the end of the season, there can be ten or more. The cells' openings face downwards. In this strange world, the young lay about drowsily, and receive their food in an upside-down position. To aid the service of the young, the open spaces are separated into tiers by linking colonnades. Here, the wet nurses come and go incessantly, busy with their larvae. Lateral trap doors between the exterior wall and the stacks of cells provide easy access from all directions. Finally, on the side of envelope, the door to the city opens with little architectural grandeur, a modest opening lost beneath the sheets of the surrounding wall. Opposite is the lobby leading to the outside world.

The cells of the lower layers are larger than those in the upper layers. They are reserved as nurseries for the males and queens, while the upper layers house the worker wasps, slightly smaller. In the beginning, the community requires worker wasps in great numbers. These celibate wasps are entirely devoted to work, helping to build the nest, and transform it into a flourishing city. Concerns for future perpetuation come later. More spacious cells are constructed, intended partly for the males, partly for the queens. Based on the numbers, I would estimate that the sexual population accounts for roughly a third of the total. In a completed nest, the total number of cells can reach thousands. For each layer, the count is roughly a hundred. Despite my numerical flexibility, my result concords very well with that of Réaumur, who counted 16,000 cells in a nest of 15 layers. The master adds: with 10,000 cells, each of which are likely to each play host to three successive larvae, a wasp nest can produce more than 30,000 wasps in a year.

PAPER WASP (*Polistes gallicus*)
on its nest.

spanish fly

PAIR OF MATING BEETLES of the Cantharidae family (*Rhagonycha* sp.) on a blade of grass.

H ere is a curious story to write: love in the insect world. The subject has tempted me in the past. For a quarter of a century, my notes lay, dusty, in a recess of my archives. I have extracted what follows on the Spanish Fly, a green beetle. I am not the first, I know, to describe the amorous preludes of beetles; but with a different narrator, the narration can still have value. It confirms that which has already been said, and illuminates some points that had perhaps not been raised.

A female Spanish Fly chews peacefully on a leaf. A lover appears, approaching her from the back, abruptly climbs onto her back and clasps her with his two pairs of hind legs. With his abdomen, which he stretches as much as possible, he thrashes against the female, to the left and to the right. These blows are delivered at a frenetic pace. With his free antennae and front legs he flogs the patient female's nape. The blows coming down like hail, from the front and the back, the head and the breast of the enamoured one are oscillating in an uncoordinated frenzy. If we did not know better, the behaviour could be mistaken for an epileptic attack.

CHAFER (*Oxythyrea funesta*) on an iris flower.

ROSE CHAFER (*Cetonia aurata*) on an artichoke flower.

The female is being dominated; she parts her wing cases slightly, hides her head and folds the lower part of her abdomen, as if to remove herself from the erotic storm taking place on her back. The onrush calms. The male stretches his front legs in the form of a cross, in a nervous and lustful movement. The antennae and the belly become still, stretched out straight; but the head and the breast continue their rapid up-and-down oscillation. This time of relative rest does not last for long. The female, whose appetite seems untroubled by the heated protests of her suitor, goes back to nibbling her leaf.

Another onrush is unleashed. The blows rain down again on the entangled insect's nape and again she hurries to bend her head under her chest. He ignores her attempts to hide. With his front legs, aided by a special notch at the joint of the leg and the tarsus, he seizes both of her antennae. The tarsus folds and the antenna is held in place, as if in a claw. The suitor pulls her back towards him, and so she is forced to lift her head. In this position, the male reminds me of a knight proudly mounted on his horse, holding the reins in both hands. The female, after having thrashed about frenetically, now remains still for a moment.

Rose Chafer (*Cetonia aurata*) on a Woolly Thistle flower.

Then, with his long abdomen, the male pokes at her, also striking her gently with his antennae, head and legs. The object of desire would be cold-hearted to not return such a warm declaration. He continues to solicit her. Then the passionate male reassumes his ecstatic stillness, his quivering arms in cross formation. In short intervals, the amorous passions start again. They begin with the carefully dealt blows, followed by the resting period during which the male spreads his front legs to form a cross or else controls the female by the bridle of her antennae. Finally, the battered female succumbs to the charms of his blows. She gives in. The mating takes place and lasts about twenty hours. The male's role is complete.

Now, dragged backwards while still attached to the female's backside, the unhappy male tries hard to break up the pairing. His companion carts him from leaf to leaf, wherever it pleases her, to find a piece of greenery to suit her tastes. Sometimes, he also wisely takes advantage of this to nibble like the female. Perhaps, so as not to miss out of an instant of their four to five weeks of life, they take it upon themselves to fulfil the appetites of the heart and of the stomach at the same time – their motto is surely: 'Short and sweet'.

MALE STAG BEETLE (*Lucanus cervus*)
on the branch of an oak tree.

GREAT CAPRICORN BEETLE (*Cerambyx cerdo*)

The larva of the Capricorn Beetle eats everything in its path. With its carpenter's gouge, its robust, short, black mandibles, shaped like sharp-edged spoons, it eats through the heart of an oak tree. The mouthful it has carved out will yield its meagre juices as it passes through the stomach and then accumulates behind the busy worker as waste. The organic matter involved in this work temporarily departs from the free world as it passes through the worker. A work of nutrition and road clearing, the route is eaten as it is travelled; it is obstructed behind as it is cleared in front. It is in this way that tunnelling beetle larvae achieve sustenance and shelter in their wooden home.

In spite of its sturdy appearance, an adult Capricorn Beetle could not exit the tree trunk on its own. The task falls onto the larva, in all its intestinal wisdom, to clear the paths. Under the impulse of a premonition, to our eyes an unfathomable mystery, the larva leaves the inside of the oak tree, its peaceful retreat, its impregnable fortified castle, to make its way towards the exterior. It comes close to exposing itself to the enemy, the woodpecker, who would delight in eating the succulent grub. In this dangerous situation it digs tenaciously, eating into the tree, until it reaches the bark, which it chews to a paper-thin curtain. Sometimes the reckless creature even creates a window.

Here sits the Capricorn Beetle larva at its opening. The adult insect will only have to file down the curtains slightly with the ends of its mandibles, or hit the window with its brow to knock it down. It will have nothing at all to do if the window is open, as is often the case. The unskilled carpenter, encumbered by its extravagant panache, will emerge from the darkness of the opening when the hot days arrive.

PAIR OF MATING LONGHORN BEETLES (*Agapanthia* sp.)
on a thistle.

small world of εntomology

'Our knowledge of plants is as old as our infirmities and our need for food. Our knowledge of insects is, on the contrary, very recent. We have a vague understanding of the work of the bee and the silkworm; we have heard of the ant's industrious behaviour; we know the cicada song without having a precise idea of the singer, confused with others; we have perhaps taken a distracted glimpse at the magnificence of butterflies; entomology can be reduced to this for the vast majority of the population.'

Jean-Henri Fabre

Left to right:

PAIR OF MATING SEVEN-SPOT LADYBIRDS
(*Coccinella septempunctata*)

SIX-SPOT BURNET MOTH
(*Zygaena filipendulae*) gathering nectar on a
bramble flower.

COLORADO BEETLE (*Leptinotarsa decemlineata*)
laying its eggs on a potato plant leaf.

LONGHORN BEETLE (*Leptura cordigera*)
on a bramble flower.

CRICKET (*Calliptamus* sp.)
on a marjoram flower in a meadow.

autumn

Pair of mating Praying Mantises (*Mantis religiosa*) on an amaranth leaf.

PRAYING MANTIS (*Mantis religiosa*)

Such fierce creatures! Wolves are said not to eat their own kind, but the female mantis shows no such restraint. She delights in consuming her equal, when crickets, her favourite prey, abound around her. Her actions are equivalent to cannibalism, one of the most appalling crimes known to man.

These urges of this maternal creature can reach even more revolting heights. Let's assist the pairing, and to avoid overgeneralization, let's isolate the couples under different situations. Each pair has its own mating ground, where no-one would dare interrupt the marriage. Let's not forget the food supply, which is still abundant, so as not to justify the excuse of hunger. It is near the end of August. The slender male lover perceives that the time is right. He winks at his powerful companion; he turns his head on its side, bends his neck, and sticks out his chest. His little pointed face almost seems to express passion. In this pose, completely still, he gazes at his object of affection. She does not move, seeming indifferent. The lover, however, has detected a signal of agreement, one to which I do not hold the secret.

PAIR OF MATING PRAYING MANTISES
(*Mantis religiosa*) on an amaranth leaf.

PRAYING MANTIS (*Mantis religiosa*), the female eats her mate.

He draws closer; suddenly he spreads out his wings, they quiver convulsively. This is his declaration. He dashes up onto the back of his corpulent mate. He holds on tightly as well as he can, stabilizing himself. Generally, preludes go on for long periods. Finally the mating takes place, a lengthy process as well, up to five or six hours at times. There is little to sustain interest in the immobile pair. Finally they separate, but they will reunite soon, in an even more intimate way. If the poor creature is cherished by the female for bringing life to her ovaries, he is also beloved as a most exquisite meal. Within the day or the next at the latest, he is seized by his companion, who first gnaws into his nape, following the usual custom, and then methodically, in small mouthfuls, consumes him, leaving nothing but the wings. This is not jealously between equals, but depraved hunger.

Curiosity led me to wonder how a second male would be received by the fertilized female. The result of my inquiry is scandalous. The mantis, in many cases, is never satisfied by its love-making and conjugal feasts. After a varying amount of rest, the laying having already occurred or not, a second male is accepted, and is devoured like the first. A third succeeds him, plays its part and is eaten as well. A fourth goes in the same manner. In the interval of two weeks, I have witnessed the same female mantis go through up to seven males. To each she offers herself, from each she takes his life in exchange.

MATING PAIR OF PRAYING MANTISES (*Mantis religiosa*)

PRAYING MANTIS (*Mantis religiosa*)
building her egg mass on some old wooden fence-posts.

WOLF SPIDER (*Hogna radiata*)

The Wolf Spider shares the mentality of the cricket; it is a wanderer by nature. Towards September its nuptial readiness is visible as a badge of black velour on the belly. At night, under the soft light of the moon, the pair meet, they woo, and share a small meal after the marriage. During the day, they travel the country to track down prey in the carpet of short grass, and partake in the joys of the sunshine. It is a much more worthy existence than meditating alone at the bottom of a well. It is not rare to encounter young mothers which have not established a dwelling, weaving their egg sac or even taking care of their young family.

In October, it is time to settle down. We find essentially two types of dens, differing in diameter. The larger one, the size of a bottle neck, belongs to the old matrons, proprietors of the dwelling for at least two years. The smaller ones, roughly the size of a heavy pencil, house the young mothers born in the preceding year. With their many alterations, undertaken at leisure, the first-time mothers' dwellings will expand in depth and diameter to become spacious homes, like those of their seniors. In each, we find the proprietor with her family, either hatched or still enclosed in the satin bag.

As they have no gardening implement that seemed up the

THE WOLF SPIDER'S (*Hogna radiata*) impressive mandibles.

task of excavating the dwelling, I wondered whether the Wolf Spider would take advantage of a fortuitous burrow, the work of a cicada or earthworm. Such a burrow, I thought, would shorten the arachnid's dig, for which it appears so ill-equipped. All that would be required is to enlarge it and even it out. I was mistaken: from the entrance to the very bottom, the spider digs the entire tunnel from scratch. Where are its boring tools? We would suspect its legs or its claws, but upon further reflection, it becomes clear that such tools, too long and difficult to handle in narrow spaces, would be insufficient. What we need here is the miner's short-handled pick to strike hard. A sharp point is needed to plunge into the earthy mass, causing it to crumble into

bits. That leaves the Wolf Spider's fangs, fine weapons that we would hesitate to ascribe to this line of work, in the same way that it seems illogical to dig a well with a scalpel. They are two sharp curved points, bent like a curved finger at rest, which are sheltered between two strong pillars. The cat retracts its claws over the pads of its paws, so as to protect their sharpness. In much the same way, the Wolf Spider protects its poisonous daggers by folding them under the shelter of two heavy columns that descend from the face, containing the muscles responsible for their movement. This surgical kit, designed to arrest its prey, is used in this instance as a pick for the crude task of digging.

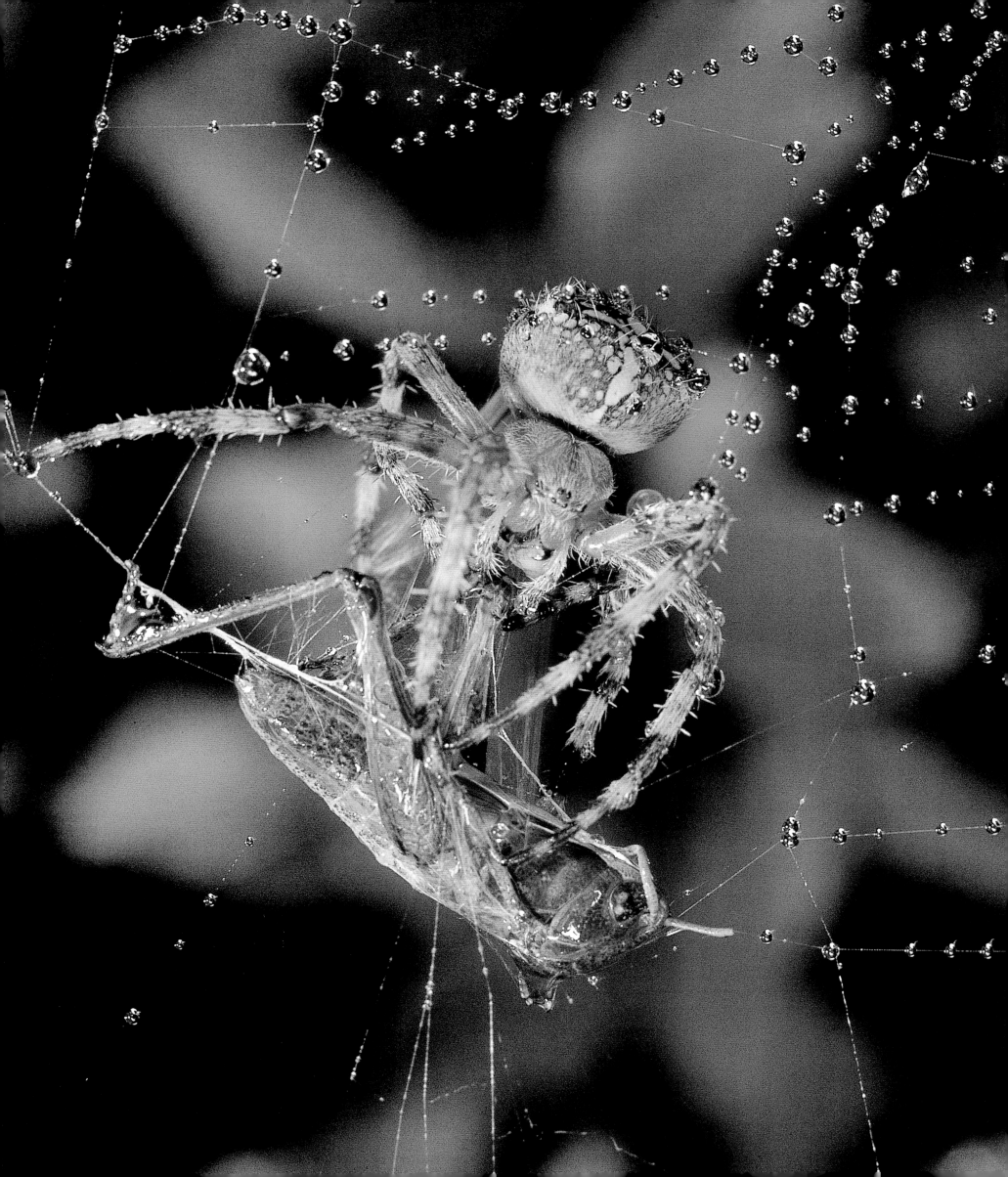

Wasp Spider (*Argiope bruennichi*) injecting poison, after having wrapped a grasshopper.

The Garden Spider cannot choose what it will capture. Immobile at the centre of its web with its eight feet spread so as to sense shocks in the network in all directions, it waits for what chance will deliver it. Perhaps the first prey will be a dizzy fly that has not yet mastered its flight, the next a sturdy grasshopper having taken an ill-considered leap. The impetuous cricket in particular, prone to adventurous release of its spring-like thighs, frequently falls into the trap. Its vigour would seem imposing to the arachnid; with the bucking of its powerful legs you would think it capable of quickly tearing up the web. It is nothing like this. If it can't free itself in its first effort, the cricket is doomed.

Turning its back to its prey, the Garden Spider spews forth silk from all its spinnerets like a showerhead. The silky fountain is gathered by the hind legs, which are longer than the others, opening fully in an arc to lighten the discharge. Using this technique, it is no longer a thread that the spider has at its disposal, but rather a shimmering sheet, a cloudy fan whose threads remain nearly independent. As this is happening, the two hind legs direct the silk alternately, while turning and rotating the prey to swaddle it on all sides.

The ancient Roman retiarius gladiator, fighting against a powerful big cat, enters the arena with a net folded over his shoulder. The beast pounces. The man, with a quick movement of his right hand, spreads the web like a trained fisherman; covering the animal and tangling it in the mesh. A strike of the trident and the match is won.

Garden Spider (*Araneus diadematus*)
wrapping a cricket.

spider's poison

WEB OF A GARDEN SPIDER (*Araneus diadematus*) in an autumn meadow.

The Garden Spider behaves in a similar manner, with the advantage of having a supply of extra nets. If the first load does not suffice, a second instantly follows and then another and another, until the silk reserves are exhausted.

When nothing moves under the white shroud, the spider approaches the bound prey. It has a better weapon than the gladiator's trident: its venomous fangs. It bites the cricket, and then pulls back, leaving the victim to weaken in torpor. Soon it returns to the prey's motionless body. It sucks at the cricket, drying it out, sometimes moving to suck from a different part of the cricket's body. Finally the remains of the former insect, bled white, is thrown away, and the spider resumes its vigil at the centre of the web.

It is not a cadaver that the Garden Spider has sucked, but a benumbed creature. If I take the cricket from the web immediately after the bite and remove the silk sheath, the surgical victim resumes its normal vigour so well that it seems to not to have been subjected to any harm. The spider therefore does not kill its captive before drinking its juices; it contents itself with rendering it motionless by torpor. The benign nature of the bite perhaps provides greater ease in sucking the bodily fluids. Stagnant in a corpse, the fluids would become less suited to the sucker; its extraction is easier when they are still moving in a living being.

WASP SPIDER (*Argiope bruennichi*)
on its dew-covered web.

178

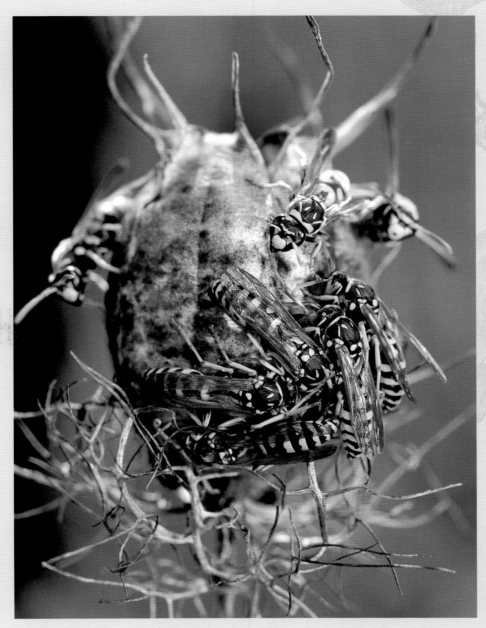

PAPER WASPS (*Polistes gallicus*) taking refuge on a Love-in-a-mist capsule, after having their nest attacked by a European Hornet.

Two conditions seem to have precipitated the collapse of the nest. When the winter arrives, the wasp nest empties itself due to famine and cold. In winter, there is no more food, no more sweet fruits, primary food source of the wasps. In spite of their shelter, the frost finishes off the starving insects. Is this the end of the nest? We shall see.

Death, even if it be that of a single wasp, is always a serious thing, worthy of our attention. Day by day, I observe with an unsettling curiosity the last days of my creatures. One detail in particular strikes me: the worker wasps succumb rather suddenly. They come to the surface, let themselves slide, fall on their backs and don't get up again, as if struck dead by lightening. They have put in their time. They are killed by age, in all its inexorable toxicity. Like a spring having delivered its last bounce, it is rendered inert.

HORNET (*Vespa crabro*) extracting the larvae
from a Paper Wasp nest (*Polistes sp*).

181

However, the queen females, last wasps to be born in the city, far from being condemned to decay, are only just beginning their lives. They possess the vigour of youth. When the troubles of winter come, they are capable of resisting, while the old workers perish so abruptly. It is the same situation with the males. Until their role is completed, they resist quite well. The females whose end is approaching are easily distinguished from the others by their neglected appearance. Their backs are dusty. The healthy females, after having had their meal on the side of the honey pot, sit in the sun and continually dust themselves. The sickly, not preoccupied with grooming, sit motionless in the sun or wander

sluggishly. They give up on brushing themselves. This lack of care is portentous. Two or three days later, the dusty female exits the wasp nest one last time, and sits on the roof to enjoy the sun a little longer. Then, the claws lose their strength and cease to support her, and softly she falls to the ground, never to get up again. She does not want to die in the cherished paper dwelling, where the wasps' code imposes strict cleanliness.

If the workers were still there, staunch hygienists that they are, they would apprehend the infirm insect and drag her outside. But they were the first victims of the winter's wrath; in their absence, the moribund queen takes on her own funeral by

WASP SPIDER (*Argiope bruennichi*) on its web.

letting herself fall into the mass grave below. For reasons of sanitation, an indispensable condition in such high numbers, these stoics refuse to pass away between the layers of their home. It is a law that is never repealed, however reduced the nest's population may be. All dead bodies must be discarded from the young wasps' dormitory.

The various nests visited towards the end of December all show the same mortality. The queens perish nearly in an equal numbers to the rest of the population. It is to be expected. The number of females, daughters of the same wasp nest, is unknown to me. However, the abundance of their bodies in the colony's mass grave is telling. They must number hundreds and hundreds,

perhaps even thousands. One queen is sufficient to found a city of thirty thousand inhabitants – if they all thrived, what a scourge they would be! Wasps would hold tyrannical control over the countryside.

Order would have it that the vast majority perish, killed not by an accidental epidemic and inclement weather of the season, but by an inevitable fate that seeks to destroy the desire to procreate. So a question arises: since a solitary wasp, surviving by some means, is all that is required to sustain the species, why have so many aspiring mothers in the wasp nest? Why the mass as opposed to the singular? Why so many victims? It is a troubling question, which our understanding fails to answer.

Praying Mantis (*Mantis religiosa*) cleaning its feet.

Young Conehead Mantis (*Empusa pennata*)
on a Teasel flower in autumn.

A CICADA'S (*Cicada orni*) empty larval casing or exuvium attached to a blade of grass.

LILY BUSH CRICKET (*Tylopsis lilifolia*)
on a dried Teasel flower.

index